Stories
Christi

A Girl's
Best Friend

Series editor: Judith Baxter

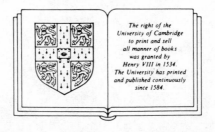

The right of the
University of Cambridge
to print and sell
all manner of books
was granted by
Henry VIII in 1534.
The University has printed
and published continuously
since 1584.

CAMBRIDGE UNIVERSITY PRESS

Cambridge   New York   Port Chester
Melbourne   Sydney

Published by the Press Syndicate of the University of Cambridge
The Pitt Building, Trumpington Street, Cambridge CB2 1RP
40 West 20th Street, New York, NY 10011, USA
10 Stamford Road, Oakleigh, Melbourne 3166, Australia

Supplementary material © Cambridge University Press 1990

First published 1987 by The Women's Press Ltd
First published in this edition by Cambridge University Press 1990

rinted in Great Britain by Redwood Press Limited, Melksham, Wiltshil

British Library Cataloguing in Publication Data
A Girl's Best Friend
I. Dunhill, Christina
823.0108[FS]

ISBN 0 521 38560 1

GO

Contents

Introduction

Christina Dunhill

This book grew out of what was at first an idea for a collection of love stories. There were three of us working for The Women's Press on their Livewire series for teenage readers. We decided together that we should advertise for stories by young women writers about relationships – all the different relationships which are important in a girl's life. When the stories came in, I was surprised that hardly any of them turned out to be about romance. On the other hand, they're all about love in one way or another.

We were looking for stories which were both honest and real. We wanted freshness and frankness – nothing sentimental. It's up to you to judge how far we succeeded. It hardly needs saying that we wanted stories from women of different backgrounds: racial, class and geographical. Six of the stories here, for example, are by Black women.

This is a collection for teenage girls: no bones about it. For boys who read it, I hope you get something out of it. You are only doing what girls have always been ready to do, in identifying with heroes of the opposite sex.

Some of the stories are by women in their twenties: Millie Murray, Jill Dawson, Jenneba Sie Jalloh, Esther Bloom, Sandra Agard. Tracy Vidal was only sixteen when she wrote hers. But from all the writers, we were looking for the ability to be in touch with their teenage years – years which are so important but the memory of which may get 'furred up' as you grow older, more comfortable and closed in.

Perhaps it's no surprise that so many of the stories are about parents, given the amount of time young people spend with them. In some stories, the parents come off well; in others, they don't. In Sandra Agard's story, it's her overworked and sharp-talking mum who sorts out the meaning of her sleepless nights. Janice Galloway's *First Foot* is about a mother who resists all her daughter's attempts to please her. In Tracy Vidal's *Funny How Time Flies*, the shadow of Kim's parents' impending divorce looms over the humour. In Sigrid Nielsen's *The Night Run*, both girls have to cope with parents who are not on their wavelength. Jill Dawson's story is about how a young girl feels when her father brings his 'fancy woman' home to their New Year's Eve Party. Perhaps the story which focuses most on love for a parent is Jenneba Sie Jalloh's beautiful and painful tribute to a dead father.

Other stories are about girlfriends. Sigrid Nielsen's deep and moving *The Night Run* revolves round a friendship arising from a mutual passion for science fiction. I particularly like the fact that its last lines are the ending for the whole book:

P.S. I don't know if I want to be called The Keeper of Crystalcant.

I think I would rather be called something like Black Lightning.

P.P.S. You are the only friend I've ever had.

Barbara Jacobs's story tackles the painful business of making friends again after a girl lets a holiday romance get in the way of a long-standing friendship. Esther Bloom's story is about a girl persuading her sister to do her a favour. Girlfriends are the day-to-day life: they offer fun, humour and support – in between the rows.

Unexpected friendships between girls and older women also play a part in the book. Tracy Vidal's Kim is sent on a do-gooding mission by her school to visit an old lady. Kim plays truant the next day so that she can visit the old lady again. In Kerilyn Wood's story, Jen gets cheered up in hospital by the rude and boisterous chatter of Flo and Mrs. Rice.

Only Mary Hooper's *Once Upon A Time* is really a romance. It appears to be a spoof except that Liz's fantasy about a boy comes true, despite herself. The boy in Janice Galloway's story is her best friend but nobody understands this. Her mother thinks that she should get herself a proper boyfriend and stop 'getting a name about herself' by hanging around with him. Ravi Randhawa's Sunni falls in love, but part of Firoz's importance is that he helps her in developing her political awareness. The main thrust of the story is about racism and what happened in Southall in 1979.

Humour is important to many of these stories. Some of them are written as funny stories: those by Esther Bloom, Tracy Vidal, Barbara Jacobs, Mary Hooper and Kate Hall (about which nothing is said or it would spoil it). But it's a fine line. The funny stories are also serious. The serious stories have their comic moments. One important aspect is backchat. This is Ravi Randhawa's group of friends responding to a young man asking them for help on his paper. 'We haven't got any women,' he says. They say:

'We don't do it for money . . .'
'Pleasure is all we want . . .'
'Most blokes can't give either . . .'

And here are Barbara Jacobs's two friends 'lipping' two boys who have been sizing them up while walking behind them:

'Oi! Girls! How about a chip?' . . .
'Not keen on the legs, Lisa,' I sighed.
'What legs? I don't see any legs. They're on castors.'

Introspection, fantasy and secret life are also key features. Jenneba Sie Jalloh's *Always Remembered* is partly written through diary entries to a made-up friend called Teresa. In Mary Hooper's story, the humour comes from the contrast between Liz's fantasy life of Sassoon haircuts, fast cars and ritzy clubs, and her real-life visit to the disco at the village hall.

The lights are low, the carpets thick, the decor luxuriously understated, I sink into a small gold chair and let the music surround me in a smooth bank of sound . . .

'Hey!' Emma is shaking my arm. 'I said, shall we sit near the stage or near the loo?'

In *The Night Run*, Catriona writes stories about herself, partly out of loneliness. She imagines herself as a heroic character in a brighter, braver sci-fi world. When she meets Anne, she writes her new friend into the stories, and this is part of the force which holds the friendship together.

Central to all the stories in one way or another is growing up and thinking things out for yourself. In *Sunni* and *Seeing for Herself*, this means the courage to believe in your own convictions and to make up your own mind. Issues of identity and pride are very much part of this. In the Black women's stories, these issues are bound up closely with racial awareness – the idea that you do not act simply as an individual, but as a member of a particular racial group within society. Tracy Vidal, who is Black, is perhaps the exception in choosing not to write specifically about this.

The stories here are both funny and serious and I hope you enjoy them. Also, I hope they may encourage you to think more about writing yourselves. Some of the stories come straight from the writers' experiences. Others are made up. Whichever approach you use, draw from your own life and write about what you know. In that way, even if you *are* making it up, it will have *truth*. This is the important quality in writing, and this is what we hope *A Girl's Best Friend* has to offer.

Funny How Time Flies (When You're Having Fun)

Tracy Vidal

'Mummy and Daddy don't love each other any more.' I speak softly and lower my body to her height. 'They do love you. I promise.' I think. 'They just don't get on any more.'

Shauna squirms and screws up her four-year-old face.

Am I making sense?

'I want to see Mummy NOW!'

'She's gone out,' I answer.

I get up and go back to my desk. Patience is a virtue.

With a teddy bear hugged tightly to her chest, she climbs on to her bed. She faces me and watches, a wall of tears behind her frightened eyes. She acknowledges what I've said.

I want to give comfort.

I look down at my homework. It stares up at me with blank oppression. The blue biro is in my hand, the date scrawled on the top of the page of the exercise book. I'd better get on.

Divorce. I know what my hand has written but since nothing and nobody can control what I write but me, I take as much time as I want. I feel a longing for something, I can't grasp what. D–I–V–O–R–C–E. *My name is* (perhaps I should stay anonymous) *Kim.*

Hi! I'm thirteen years old. I have a younger sister, Shauna, who is four and an eighteen-year-old brother, Duane.

My eyes roll upward and collide with the ceiling at the thought. Nothing can describe his selfishness. He

1

stays in his room and never talks to us mere mortals. Unemployment was made for him. At times, I could do him a serious GBH.

But it's not him who's the actual problem. It's my parents. They are getting a divorce because they do not get on any more. It happens! Honest!

I go to the hook on the door, to my coat. I grope around in the deep crevasse of the pocket and dig out a can of coke.

'Can I have some?'

'No. Go back to sleep.'

Dad's late. I know even without checking the time. That's why Mum isn't in. Dad's coming round. His moving out was through mutual agreement.

Suddenly *Hill Street Blues* springs to mind and I reach for the newspaper on the floor. It's been cancelled for football. Can you beat that? I put it down and look up to the clock. 21.03 p.m.

I had to cook dinner today. Oven chips, beans and sausages. I can't cook. Mum's been out all day and Dad's late. I haven't really concentrated on my home-work. There's a logical reason to this.

'Wanna go wee-wee.'

I raise my eyes from the page. Shauna's face punctures the pillow and her feet stamp a repetitive mumble on the mattress. Her body's arched and her backside looks suspended in the air, held up by some new form of gravity. There's a first.

I pick her up to save time, and carry her to the bathroom where she holds on to the cold black seat for dear life. We march back piggyback style.

'Why don't Mummy and Daddy get on?' Her chin bounces on my shoulder.

'I don't know. What I told you is what they told me. See?'

'See.'

I don't suppose they did it on purpose – the divorce, I

2

mean. However, life goes on. I guess they forgot they've got kids. It's understandable, not everyone has an impeccable memory.

I put Shauna back to bed. She's a heavy sleeper but I try to make as little noise as possible. We share a room.

My homework is for a new teacher. She wants us to write an essay describing ourselves. I shan't proceed to tell you how many of those I've done since the first year.

It's getting late now. This is bloody ridiculous.

I just remembered. A girl at school, Andrea, was talking about a disco tonight. Shit. I'd better shut up. Jealousy will get me nowhere.

22.03 pm

I unscrew the Tippex, keeping its infuriating reek as far away as possible. '*Divorce*' disappears along with the rest under the thick white coat. I'll change while it dries.

A large yawn escapes. Ah well.

I plod around in my new shoes as I pick up the odd book, toy and item of clothing off the floor. It's great how these shoes match my nightshirt.

I check to see if Shauna is asleep. Silly thing to do. The heavy breathing says it all.

I've been in bed for ten glorious minutes and I've just remembered my homework. I won't save it for tomorrow because I know it won't get done. There's a premonition for you.

22.31 p.m.

Kim is an ordinary name and I am an ordinary person. (I am also an individual.)

It's warm under the blankets. My eyelashes are entwined in an effort to sleep. I can't see anything, it's dark. I stretch my body over the single bed and try to imagine sleep. I know it's waiting for me, deep in my mind. If I think about it, my thoughts will disappear and sleep will be there, and my dream.

3

But my mind is buzzing. I want to open my eyes and start again but the murky grey form of the chair in the corner frightened me *last* night. I turn on to my stomach. I can feel the darkness screaming at me. Fog-like clouds drift into my mind. Thoughts of Ricky float in with them. He's nice. But. My parents are standing there like a barrier, shaking their heads. I can't even ask why.

I cannot see me. I shudder. Ricky has gone from the picture in my mind. My parents remain. There I am! I'm walking away . . . I stop and look back. I want to run, run as far away as possible, but my feet won't move and my reflexes refuse to work. I grab the pillow and bury my head under it. I can't escape.

Then my friend, Joanne, appears. She doesn't see me.

'Kim!' she calls. 'Kim, are you coming to the disco?'

For once, my parents agree, both shaking their heads.

'Kim? Kim?' She fades into nothing.

Ricky Gorman. He goes to my school. I think he's cute. To tell the truth, absolutely gorgeous. I sent him a valentine card. I don't think he likes me the way I like him, though. Better luck next time. My parents are standing there . . . Maybe he really does want to ask me out. But my parents are still standing there. They can't sort themselves out but they can tell *me* what to do! My feet are moving. Running!

My parents are invading my private thoughts. I want to dream what *I* want. I have an identity. I am me. I want to pass my exams. I want to have fun. I want to make a go of my life. I have a choice . . . don't I?

I try to erase my thoughts, to think of sleep. If I concentrate, my thoughts will disappear and there, there will be sleep and my dream.

My eyes flicker open. I crane my neck to see the clock.

7.30 a.m.

I start my Sunday rituals.

4

First I go to make sure that Joey, the goldfish, has not gone to the big goldfish tank in the sky. He's fine. I sneak open Mum's door. She's in. Isn't that *awfully* nice of her!

I make a bowl of exceedingly soggy cornflakes and contemplate a long Radox bath. I love to coat the bath with a film of Radox before the water spills menacingly over it. Well, we all have our funny little habits.

Another boring Sunday. Hard to decide which was the high point, having a bath or staring at Joey.

The Monday morning dread of going to school whacks me square in the face. I now know how Garfield feels. You have my sympathy, comrade. School should be run by flexi-time. Inconvenience the teachers for a change.

I forgot. It's social services day in school, a kind gesture with a sly political underlying theme: 'We'll help the pensioners if you won't.' It's only done once a year but the prospect of such an act does not appeal to me in the slightest. Joanne isn't in school, too ill to perform saintly duties, so she'd told me yesterday on the phone.

Wonderful invention, the phone. Right now I'd like to use the cord for illicit purposes on Kamilla Davey, she's partnered with Ricky. My form teacher couldn't give a monkey's that I'll be playing little Red Riding Hood on my tod, but I suppose I did wind her up a bit, being TRUTHFUL about not handing my homework in. The usual 'I forgot' didn't go down too well with the girl before me so I thought I'd try new tactics to worm out of detention. I'll hand it in tomorrow. Problem solved.

I give the stiff knocker three hard blows. Obviously some people don't know what oil is for. Slippers shuffle to the door and it is pulled open. A squinting eye peers over the chain.

'Yes?'

'Kim Lewis, from Manor School.'

She continues to stare. It hasn't registered. Cor, she must think I've got all day. A succession of blinks leads to her shutting the door, releasing the chain and eventually letting me in.

Needy pensioner my foot! Her interior decor is in a better state than my nan's used to be. Then again, my tight-fisted parents did (not) contribute. She leads me into the living-room.

'What did you say your name was?' Her voice sounds gruff. A bit scary. She might have hundreds of mutilated bodies of innocent kids, like me, blocking her kitchen sink for all I know.

'Kim.'

'Want some tea?'

'Yes, please.' Why not? I prop the bag of goodies beside a chair.

Off she goes to make some good olde English cha. I look around the room. It's like the lady herself, set in her ways. You can tell the furniture hasn't been moved for ages. The usual show of school photos of her grandchildren along with a couple of seaside souvenirs and postcards of both recent Royal Weddings clutters the mantelpiece. Another photograph, almost hidden from my twenty-twenty vision, catches my eye. It is going yellow around the sides although it's black and white with a young man grinning energetically to the camera. I can only imagine that Kodak weren't around to capture that golden moment – on their famous Kodak paper just before he got fed up and frowned.

'That's my Bill.' She plonks the tray down on the table in the centre of the room. 'Never did like to be called William.' I grimace. 'Said it rolled off the tongue, a bit too posh for the East End. Sugar?'

'Two, please.'

'He died nine weeks ago this Thursday. I suppose that's why they packed you off round here. Bet you'd rather be with your mates, eh?'

Bingo.

She picks up her tea and sits down munching on a biscuit, indicating that I should do the same. She sips her tea. At least she's stopped yapping.

'My name's Bess, if you didn't know, and the dog,' I look to the small heap under the window, 'he's called Dunky.'

I grin.

'He's practically as old as I am.' She looks at me as though I'm going to contradict her. 'I'm eighty-four.' And she doesn't look a day over sixty. Wait a minute. I'm not being fair.

'I'm thirteen.'

'You've got a long way to go yet, love!'

'How many grandchildren have you got?'

'Eight. You'd never believe it though, I've only got one son.' She sits back in the armchair. 'The randy sod.'

I burst into uncontrollable laughter. She gives me that blank look, again. I don't think she's realised what she said, for a moment, then joins in. She puts down the mug and starts to cough.

'Excuse me.' Cough, splutter. 'I've got a bit of a chill.'

I stand up to pat her back and the cough stops. Magic.

'What about your family.'

No hesitation, why act abnormal? 'I've a sister who's four, a brother, eighteen, and both natural parents still alive and kicking.'

'You miserable thing you!' She refills the mugs from a spout poking out of a bright pink cosy.

'What?' I ask as innocently as I can.

'You know!' She winks. 'I thought I was bad when I was your age. A little rebel, I was. The war soon put a stop to that and I had to grow up pretty sharpish. I

7

didn't meet Bill till after, mind you . . .' She shakes her head and her body wobbles. 'Oh, why didn't you tell me to stop wittering on like that! What about your parents?'

I'm trying my utmost to keep my mouth shut about them.

'Come on,' she urges gently. Her crackly voice is warm and encouraging.

'They're getting a divorce.'

She sympathises. 'I'm sorry, love.' She doesn't want to pry.

'It's nothing exciting like adultery or partner battering. They told me they don't get on any more. Simple.'

'I've never heard such nonsense. In my day, couples stuck it out. It's a serious thing, you know.'

'Well, your view and my parents' clash. They're all at it. Divorce seems to be a bit of a trend now.'

'Don't get me wrong. Divorce is understandable and it does occur, more than necessarily in some cases, but . . .'

'They don't argue.'

She pauses. 'Maybe not in front of you.'

'Pride?' I stop and allow stillness to fill the room. 'They haven't told me much and I don't think that's fair.'

'Nothing's fair. I'm no philosopher, but give them time. I'm sure they've other problems. You seem such a nice girl. They don't have to worry about you.'

'That's it. They've practically shoved all the responsibility for my sister on to me. I've seriously considered changing my goody-goody image. It would be fun to see Mum do without her cheap babysitter. Take last weekend. Mum went out before lunchtime because she said she wanted some time alone. I offered to leave her in peace but she said even if she locked herself in the loo we'd end up bothering each other. Fair enough. My dad was supposed to come round in the evening to see us but he didn't turn up and Mum was still out. She didn't get home till . . . God knows! My brother might as well not be there.'

She sits looking at me, all sincere. I can't cope. It's nice to be cared for though.

'I had to tell my sister,' I continue at a slower pace. 'I had to tell her Mummy wasn't in so she had to make do with me, and why Daddy doesn't live with us any more.'

She doesn't reply immediately. 'You know I haven't got a real answer, but no one is ever as wise or perfect as they'd like to be. Accept that for the time being. I'll tell you love, my life has passed by without me noticing. You just don't notice the months and years slip by till you've got time on your hands.' She laughs softly. After a bit of a struggle with the armchair she gets up.

'Come with me. I'll show you something.'

We enter a room leading off the hall.

'I'm a bit of a fanatic when it comes to dolls.'

The room is full of them. Beautifully laid out. China, wood, plastic and some made out of cuddly materials.

'How come you like dolls?' I sit on a stool beneath the window.

'It's funny how time flies, but I've clung on to a bit of childhood. My sisters and I didn't have many toys. As I recall it was one between two and there were five of us! I was bang in the middle so I got left out most of the time. I love dolls, though, always have and always will.'

'They are really beautiful. Delicate and everything! You must be proud of yourself.'

' 'Course I am!'

She shuffles to one of the shelves and picks out a small Victorian doll. She looks at it fondly. 'Here,' she hands it to me. 'I want you to have it.'

'Are you sure, I mean, you don't know me or anything.'

'As a senior citizen I reserve the right to make up my

own mind!'

Grateful and astounded, I accept it. We go back and finish the last of the tea. I look at my watch.

'You've got to go so soon?'

To tell the truth, I want to stay. She leans on the sides of the armchair for support and stands up. I press the plastic bag into her hand.

'Thanks for the tea.'

'My pleasure and thank you for all this food.' She rummages around the bag. 'You youngsters have some exotic tastes!'

Dunky is still asleep.

'You will come by again, won't you?' Her voice sounds strained as I reach to the lift. 'Any time.'

I wave and the lift doors close with a jolt before I answer.

At home I am in my room, adding a bit more to my essay. It's quite late. I feel incredibly left out. Mum is arguing with Duane. She's given him an ultimatum. Either he finds a job, gives some of his dole money towards housekeeping or she's gonna chuck him out. I know which one I'll vote for.

I climb into bed and think of my new friend – unexpected friend – and my doll. Sleep hits me like a thunderbolt.

It is morning. The curtains are already open. Shauna is tugging at my pillow. She succeeds and the cold mattress finally wakes me up.

'What is it?'

She's still dressed in her pyjamas. 'I had a dream.'

'So did Martin Luther King.' I grab the pillow back and put it under my head.

'Joey had wings and he flew up to the sky.'

'Was there a rainbow?'

'No, it was dark, but I could see Joey because he's yellow.'

'Logical.'

'Anyway, Mum says you're going to be late for school.'

'Shauna!'

I wash, change and pack my bag in record time. I sweep through the front door like a hurricane. Hold on. I search for my key. Give up, knock on the door. Mum opens it. I don't bother to go any further than the kitchen door.

'Where's the tank?' I ask Mum.

'Joey passed away. I had to get rid of him before Shauna woke up.' She looked back down at her toast and mug of steaming water. He's been around for years, it's about time,' she mutters, mainly to herself.

I pass Duane on the way out. The creature from outer space surfaces! He's dressed and looking quite trendy, wow!

'Going for a job interview?'

He sneers.

I don't go to school. I'm late anyway. Maybe I should write a bit more for this essay, but I think it's about time I hand it in. I pop into the shop and buy a pot of oil. I hang around till lunchtime, buy some chips and set off to Bess's. It's my birthday tomorrow. Funny how time flies when you're having fun, eh?

Always Remembered

Jenneba Sie Jalloh

The laughs. The tears,
       The trouble
              The heartache
Moments of pleasure
       Gone forever

The shattered dignity, wounded pride
       Almost broken

Gone
       The strong man
The fighter
       Weakened

Yearning for home:
       Africa, Sierra Leone
A dream unrealised
       (till now)

Lifelong ambition, unfulfilled
Lifelong ambition, by others ignored
Never returned to country adored.

Dee awoke with a start. She had been dreaming of her father again. She turned to the clock on her bedside table to check the time, four forty-five a.m. Then she turned to the window. A shaft of cold sharp early morning sunlight filtered through the cracks in the blind . . . dreaming about her father again. She thought back to the time of her father's death and remembered conversations with schoolfriends about dreams and dreaming. A couple had told her that when you dreamt about the dead it meant they were calling you. She shuddered . . . 'Pull yourself together Dee, and don't be stupid. If you dream about Dad it means he just wanted to say "Hullo, how's life?". . .'

Anyway, it was a nice dream. In most of the dreams she had about Sam he hadn't really died at all, just gone away somewhere (usually 'inside'). Once, when she had been on one of her many diets, her father had appeared in all sorts of weird places. Like McDonald's or taking her order behind a Kentucky Fried Chicken counter. Dee was wide awake now and it would be no use trying to get back to sleep. She contemplated a cup of tea but on second thoughts decided against it. The kitchen was too far, and she'd probably be peeing for the rest of the morning and then there would be no hope at all of getting even a nap.

She rolled on to her belly leaning over the side of the bed, stretching her arm underneath, feeling for a notebook or some paper, something to write her dream down on. Her hand felt its way to a small suitcase. She pulled it out nearly falling out of bed as she did so. She let forth a slight scream, smiled, steadied herself and turned her bedside light on.

The case was full to the brim with papers and old photographs, and almost hidden away in a corner under an old play programme, she spotted four hard covered books – her diaries – where she used to write pretend letters to an imaginary friend. She lifted out the first book she could reach and opened it. It began . . .

13 May 1979

Dear Teresa,

God!!!! What a fortnight this has been! First let me tell you that Daddy is dead. And, oh boy, what a funeral!

. . . Dee re-read the first two lines and paused on the word 'dead'. It seemed so cold, feelingless almost. Maybe children did have the best way but that wasn't how she remembered it now. Things must become distorted as time goes by, especially memories of the d——, those who've gone. She rolled on to her back, put her knees up, placed the open diary across her chest and closed her eyes. It all happened seven years ago . . .

She hadn't lived with her father, not since the age of six or seven when her mother and father had officially separated, but Dee and her father remained close. There was a feeling of mutual respect and admiration as well as an abundance of love and she would often call at his house after school, or on Saturdays.

Sundays she spent with her mother. They (her mother and herself) would eat breakfast together, something which rarely if ever happened during the week, then potter around before watching the Sunday film.

When she turned thirteen she had begun to listen to Tony Williams' 'Reggae Time' on the radio and subject her mother to the sounds issuing forth. As she got older her mother would eat her lunch accompanied by the bass line of Sly and Robbie or the melodious sounds of Carol Thompson. Her mother suffered, as she later came to realise, in silence.

Dee and her mother would make the weekly journey to church, six o'clock mass. She enjoyed church and during her 'holy period', as she liked to describe it, a phase not uncommon among Catholic girls, she would read during the service. A pious teenager. She smiled to herself as another image entered her mind, that of a book safely secured inside her prayer sheet. One could only take 'holiness' so far, even an aspiring nun. After church they would stop off at the local shop. Dee would watch as a large majority of the congregation made their way into the public house opposite. So her Sundays were always well planned and spent with her mother. Things had stayed that way until she reached fourteen.

The older she got the closer to her father she had become. What he represented in her life was of the utmost importance. He didn't, as many fathers do, represent security and a safe home (her mother did that). His image was of a more romantic nature. Now, looking back, she saw ever more clearly the extent and depth of that image. She would have forgiven him practically anything and frequently did. Life when he was around was never uncomplicated, she laughed as much as she cried. It had been a very mixed and unpredictable bag . . .

8 February 1977

Dear Teresa,

I went to Dad's this morning. When I got there he wasn't in but a few minutes later he came up the stairs. He was drunk. He told me that he had just come from the hospital because someone had kicked him in the heart, and that he had discharged himself. I told him to sit down and I'd make him some coffee, have a sleep and that he'd feel better when he woke up. I couldn't say he was drunk, cos if there's one thing Dad hates it's to be told he's drunk when he *is* drunk. He told me he didn't want coffee or sleep, that he had a knife in his pocket and he wanted to 'cut the man up'. I gave up. In the end I left and he got dressed to go somewhere but before I left he kissed me and told me not to worry. I ignored the kiss and told him not to call me if he ended up in hospital for good. He laughed and told me well in that case he'd stay out of trouble. I gave him one of my 'I don't believe you as far as I can throw you' looks and he laughed again. Seriously Teresa, I don't know what to do with him . . . he'll be the death of me.

Love,
Dee

Her father had been the only male figure she knew who wasn't a friend or someone from school. She had no brothers, uncles, grandfathers or cousins (of any significance). He was all she had in that department and likewise she was all he had, the only person living that loved him and kept giving love unquestioningly and completely without reserve. Whatever the psychological or emotional hurt or embarrassment he inflicted upon her through his drinking she forgave him. Simply because he was her father. He belonged to her. That was enough. He fulfilled all the roles and it sometimes confused even him. He enjoyed the protectiveness and teasing as much as she did. The two ran side by side with him, he could never decide which to concentrate on. Something told him, and he instinctively felt it, that he must protect, guide and warn. But at the same time he couldn't resist the jokes. . .

10 April 1977

Dear Teresa,

Daddy said last night that if I went anywhere near Peter James that he would kill me. He said that he was one of those 'bad boys' and no good for me. He told me never to get involved with a Jamaican or a Nigerian. I asked him why. He said don't worry about that, just take his word for it. He *knows* them. What he knows, whatever it is, sounds terrible. It's

17

strange because he told me before that Peter was a nice kid. Daddy then said he didn't want me to wind up on All Saints' Road. He looked really serious. I've never really seen him that serious before, except for when he's playing cards with the 'boys' or sorting his African tobacco into separate little polythene bags and mixing in the bird seed, then he looks serious.

He looked at me, smiled, then stroked my hair. It felt so good . . . he doesn't do things like that very often. I could have sat there all night listening to him but he had to go to the club. I told him not to worry, that I was going to be a lawyer and he smiled again.

Love,
Dee

12 April 1977

Dear Teresa,

Today I heard from one of my friends, whose cousin goes out with Peter James' sister, that Daddy told him I'm a judo expert. I'll kill him. How will I ever be able to look Peter or anybody else in the face again!! I've never even seen judo on telly or anything!

Love,
Dee

It had all amused him so much. The fact that boys, many of whom attempted entry into 'his' club but were disallowed because they were under age, were interested in her. A sense of pride as well as a sense of amusement that his 'little girl' could cause an interest.

Her father was her only living link with Africa. He was that part of her heritage. The only blood relation she knew of the same race. If he went, so would her living link. When he did go she made efforts to keep Africa alive within herself by finding out more about his country, in books. But it wasn't the same as being told

18

firsthand. She could never find in any history book an experience that came even close to the experiences her father had related to her.

Her father had led an 'unconventional' life since he had arrived in England and it's hard to change when you start so young, especially when everyone you know, all your friends, are involved in the same lifestyle. The only answer would be a complete break, but he never made it. Sometimes when they were alone in his room together she would watch him and on those quiet occasions she saw something in his eyes. A deep sadness and something else she couldn't explain. Then he would go out to see his friends, and drink and smoke and gamble again.

Looking back with adult eyes, knowing what she knew now, she could define the look in his eyes as a look of recognition. Recognition that it was too late, and that there was nothing he could do about it. Maybe he drank because the truth of that reality was too much to bear.

His accommodation wasn't luxurious (her mother would replace that word with 'liveable') but her happiest moments were spent there. One room, two chairs. One hardback, the other an easy chair. There was a bed, wardrobe and dressing table. At one end of the room there was a cupboard door behind which stood a sink and small ringed cooker. It was usually dimly lit. Red walls and carpet with a good measure of damp to add extra colour. It was always warm. The whole effect was cavelike, smelling either of curry and rice on a good day (he always did his best to cook when she was due to visit) or stale smoke and alcohol on a normal one. But whatever the smell, whatever the day or the luck, she loved it.

She accepted the changes in the room just as she accepted the father who lived in it. Sometimes the smell and the general 'feel' of the place made her want to leave; often her father made her cry, but she always returned. To both. To clean up or brush up whatever was in need of most repair, tidying the sheets and blankets on the bed which she had sneaked out of her mother's house to bring to him when he had first moved in and had nothing, and he had accepted them. As children do, who have no choice and know no different. . .

26 September 1977

Dear Teresa,

Mr Rose cooked today . . . watery as usual. I don't know why Daddy lets him buy the food or do the cooking. He *always* buys the cheapest food, and doesn't even cook it all, most of the ingredients he takes home with him in his string bag. But Daddy just tastes the soup and says, 'Well, Mr Rose, you've done it again,' and everyone is left to their own conclusion as to what that might mean. I know what my conclusion is.

I told him that he shouldn't let Mr Rose cook, but Daddy says that he's old and needs the money. Well as far as I can see so does Daddy! The other day he told me that he asked the fishmonger for some fish heads for his cat . . . Daddy doesn't have a cat, they were for him. He was ashamed when he told me, I could see by his face, and he changed the subject quickly. I didn't know what to say either so I didn't say anything.

After dinner Daddy got Mr Rose to dye his hair black for him and the dye went everywhere, mostly in the opposite direction from Daddy's head! I asked him why he was so vain and he said he wasn't vain, just handsome, that the women liked his mop of jet black curls. Everyone laughed including Mr Rose who while laughing spilt what was left of the dye on

Daddy's new trousers. The laughing stopped soon after that.

Then Daddy dictated a letter for my grandmother in Africa to Mr Rose. He sent her forty pounds. Forty pounds he hasn't got. He sends it to her even if he has to starve to do it. I can't see the point. Why doesn't he just tell her that he hasn't got the money which he hasn't. I think she thinks he's rich, and I think that he wants her to believe it . . . grown-ups!

> Love,
> Dee

But when her father had cooked for her himself, and they ate alone, they would sit together with a plate of semolina or ground rice on the small glass-topped coffee table in front of them. They would pick up the mixture in their fingers and roll it around into neat little balls which would then be dipped into a plate of fish and okra for him or peanut butter soup for her. She would watch the sticky saliva-like okra with intent disgust and then turn happily, gratefully, to her own sweet smooth-tasting peanut butter curry. They sat contentedly, Dee getting hopelessly, happily messy, watching telly.

Then she would wait as Sam got ready to go out. A good ten minutes to clean his shoes, another twenty minutes to fix his collar and tie, pat down his hair and then arrange his trilby. Neatly, with a slight tilt. She would sit teasing him but engrossed, enjoying every minute and watching every detail. They would walk out together, Dee linking his arm tightly. He'd take her home and continue to the club.

Her mother often said that he could have owned a string of clubs instead of working in one, but Dee knew that to own a string of clubs you had to have firstly responsibility, and secondly a desire for money. Not just what money could buy and the good time that could be had with it, but an actual desire to accumulate it and want it for its own sake. Her father didn't love money and didn't even have a strong urge or desire to acquire it. If he had ever had that desire it had left him long ago, when dreams weren't realised and it was easier to soften the blow – of shattered dreams in a country which had never welcomed him – with a drink and a few friends.

As time went on she noticed that he was losing weight, his trousers didn't fit him properly and were now practically falling off him. His jumpers were looser, even his beer gut that she enjoyed punching and teasing so much was disappearing. He seemed very down but when she asked why, he told her that he was weary. There was a calm about him.

She saw him on the Thursday before it all happened. It was her mother's birthday and Dee had persuaded her to go with her to see Sam at the club. It was a happy reunion. The first time in two years that they were all together. Dee was a little jealous of the lavish attention her father poured on her mother and the way she felt left out by both of them but now, seeing it from an adult's eye, she understood without reserve. The reunion finally ended with Sam taking her and her mother into his arms and holding them to him. Dee gave him an extra hug and kissed him goodbye. It was the last time she saw him.

On the Saturday following her mother's birthday Dee went to his house. He wasn't in and his bed hadn't been slept in. She washed up, tidied up and wrote a note saying that she'd been around and would see him during the week. She wasn't worried, just a little curious. He could have been staying with a friend or any number of things. After all, he wasn't the most predictable father in the world.

Later that day Dee was at home doing her homework – well, at least her books were opened on the table in front of her. Her hand, almost by itself, was scribbling 'Dee for Peter – True Love Never Dies'. She looked out of the window . . . it was overcast, summer was coming and she laughed as she thought of the craziness of it . . . 'It's overcast, summer's coming!' There was a ring at the door and she rose quickly, thankful for the interruption. Perhaps it would be Peter. . .

On opening the door she was confronted with one of her father's friends and she immediately sensed trouble. Her father's friends never came to her mother's house – well, neither did her father. It was off limits for all of them. Something must have happened, and the expression on his face confirmed her fears.

'Hullo Steve, how's life?'

'Hullo Dee, okay.'

'Good . . .' She waited. 'Is there something wrong . . .?'

'Dee . . .'

'*What is it*? Has anything happened to my dad, Steve? Where is he? . . . Tell me!'

'He's, he's had an accident . . . he's in the hospital.'

'What hospital? How bad is it? . . . STEVE!'

'I don't know the details, you'd better go and see Anastasia. She knows more than I do.'

Dee ran at full speed to the shop. Anastasia was an old friend of her father's from back home whose shop was on the 'Front Line'. As she entered Dee could feel her heart pounding, her belly felt empty and her bladder was throbbing. The regulars who congregated there to sell their less-than-legal wares turned to her. Silence fell. The atmosphere suddenly became heavy, weighed down with whatever news she was about to hear.

Anastasia looked up, big, firm as if born on the very seat on which she sat. A mountain, an African mountain, wrapped in the dusty blue and canary yellows of home. Matriarch. She sat like a queen at court as her courtiers gathered around her, possessing as she did the unholy words that would create havoc in the heart and life of a fourteen-year-old girl.

Dee desperately wanted to take control of the situation, and herself, but the words just tumbled out in between gasps in her attempt to catch her breath and appear 'together' in front of these strangers. 'What's hap . . . happened, Anastasia, to . . . my dad?'

She looked peeved and just a touch, but only a touch, sorry. 'How do you know . . . what do you know about it? Who told you?'

'Anastasia, I don't know anything . . . Steve came and told me that my dad's in hospital . . . that he's had an . . . an accident! That's all I know. What's wrong with him? Is it serious? TELL ME, Anastasia! . . . Is it serious?'

Dee was finding it difficult to control her voice despite all her efforts. She looked around at the motley crew, some of whom fixed their eyes on her, some of whom chose to fix their eyes on anything but her. Anastasia shook her head angrily at her courtiers as if seeking their agreement.

'Boy, that Steve, why did he have to say anything? . . . but why? I don't understand.' (She shook her head in absolute disbelief.) 'He was wrong to say anything to the child . . . who told him to open his big mouth anyway? NOW look what's happened!'

'WHAT'S HAPPENED Anastasia? PLEASE tell me. . .'

Dee was still fighting to control the pleading, almost hysterical note in her voice. Anastasia was taking so long, talking so slowly, almost as if she was enjoying the suspense, the tension. Then she looked at Dee and her face assumed an expression that is sometimes seen on the faces of judges in old films, as they arrange a piece of black material over their white wig and proclaim, 'You will hereby be taken. . .' Dee imagined that she could see a glimmer of sympathy on Anastasia's face, but perhaps it was only pity.

'I'm sorry my dear . . . but your father is no longer with us.'

Blank. Complete blank. Nothing. Nothingness. No feeling. No people, no shop, no Anastasia, no father? 'Your father is no longer with us. . .' The words rang, then thundered in her head, demanding a response but there was none. YOUR FATHER . . . NO LONGER WITH US . . . WITH ME. The words shot through her like a knife. For a split second she didn't know where she was. Something sharp cut into her chest, making it difficult for her to breathe. Her whole body felt numb.

When she finally opened her eyes she screamed: 'NO!!!'

> The loss you feel
> The pain you feel
> The emptiness inside
> like a limb torn off
> A giant void. . .
> Something's missing
> That all important person
> > gone

Dee had begun to cry, her feet turned towards the door and she ran. Someone – she wasn't sure who – went after her, brought her back, tried to calm her down. Anastasia made a half-hearted attempt to comfort her. But Anastasia couldn't be on *her* side; how could she be? To tell her this in a shop full of people, strangers, with no one close to her to hold her. How *could* Anastasia be on her side? How could any of them?

She finally managed to break free of the man holding her arm. Shouting something about needing her mother, she ran from the dirty suffocating greyness of the shop into the dingy dubious brightness of the 'Front

Line', ironically named All Saints' Road. Aware of questioning eyes she ran past groups of hustling men selling their weed to those seeking fifteen minutes' escapism and a buzz. Selling their merchandise, 'their' women, but their eyes soon returned to the business at hand as their looks were but a glance, a slight interruption . . . questioning, but not really concerned.

Her pace slowed for a second as the strong whiff of sensi caught her damp nostrils, stinging her eyes not just from the sweet pungent smell but the memories of her father it brought with it. His 'African' cigarettes, or so he called them. She stood for a moment outside the Mangrove, once laughingly described by him as his second home, and let the smoke wind its way through her nostrils, seeping, stealing, into her memory.

He had told her that once, when she was a baby, her mother had tried unsuccessfully to get her to sleep and finally called Sam to see what he could do. He accepted the challenge, waited for her mother to leave the room and then waved the smoke of a spliff he was smoking over the cot. 'You just looked up and smiled.' he had said, 'No more tears. Just gurgles, as sweet as a nut, your father's daughter . . .'

For a moment Dee felt warm, warm with the sound and the memory of his voice filling her head blocking out everything else . . . deep, playful, teasing. Always coloured with pride when he talked about her. Even in front of her to his friends and to the many hundreds, or so it seemed, of 'uncles' and 'aunties' whom he said she had for a reason.

'This is your Uncle Frank.' he would say. 'If ever you're in trouble go to him. And if he sees you in the road and you're in any kind of trouble touch wood he'll say, 'Look, isn't that Sam's daughter?', and you'll be safe. The more people that know you in this area the safer you are, you hear? So say "Hullo" to your Uncle Frank . . . and don't be shy. Go on, take the money.'

Questionable logic perhaps, but Sam was no fool and neither was she. She overcame her shyness without too much hassle . . . took the money and kept a polite, discreet distance between herself and the motley characters her father with all his good intentions had thrust upon her.

But then the voice and the memory faded. She had stood there as the full and uncompromising impact of Anastasia's words and the grey coldness of the street hit her, knocking her into awareness, back into reality. She ran again. On reaching the main road she managed to hail a cab and the cabbie, on hearing her stifled sobs, asked her what was wrong. 'My . . . my dad is . . . dead . . . I just found out.' Trying to hold back the tears, but these words said by her for the very first time, and the brutal fact now forcing itself to be admitted, confronted *and* believed, made her cry aloud.

'It's all right, luv, you just go ahead and cry dear. Let it all out m'dear. . .' And she did.

They learned later that he died on the Friday following their birthday reunion and a full three days had passed before anyone knew. He had been walking down one of the streets off Ladbroke Grove on the way to St Charles' hospital, but this was also *en route* to his house so it will always be unclear what his final destination was. He had fallen. People walking past ignored him, thinking he was drunk or something. It was uncertain how long he lay there before someone finally phoned for an ambulance. One came . . . but too late . . . he died on the way to hospital. He died alone.

He had suffered a heart attack, his first and his last. She would never forget the mental image of her father so strong, collapsing in pain in the cold impersonal street. Alone. People walking over and around him as he lay there.

Can't forgive
    the world that killed him

Can't forgive
    the God that let them

Can't forgive
    the drink, the drugs, the clubs
    the 'friends', the 'boys' that used him

The country and the system
    which degraded
    then ignored him . . .

He had no identification on him. He might have been
buried in a pauper's grave and they would never have
known what happened to him, she probably thinking
that he had deserted her. But luckily one of the nurses,
or somebody, found a phone number written on a scrap
of paper and followed it up.

One morning you wake up . . . fine
    then suddenly

A sharp nothing, a poignant space
    something wrong

Something happened the day before
    then

        remember

Then
    A cry

      My father
        gone

Dee thought back to conversations when he had told her that he didn't want to grow old in England. He was only fifty-two. But fifty-two was too old to be living the type of life he was living. He must have known that he couldn't have continued much longer. Maybe that was the look she had seen in his eyes.

> Then, the anger
> Followed by enigma
>
> How could you leave me?
> How could you give up?
> Then blame God.
>
> How could you take him?
> Knowing I need him. . .?

What were his last thoughts, alone in that ambulance? Had he been conscious? Was there any desire to live at all left in his body? She would never know. Then much later comes the calm . . . but never the peace of mind. . .

She closed the book. Her room was now full of light and her eyes were slowly closing. She fought against the natural process. She really felt like tea now, pee or no pee. She looked to the wall in front of her and to the picture that hung there. A yellowing, black and white portrait of herself and her father with his 'just out of prison' haircut. A three-year-old Dee sat on one arm and a pigeon perched gracefully on the other. It was taken in Trafalgar Square. Her father was smiling, she looked terrified. Dee smiled and felt warm. She stared drowsily at her father's eyes. Smiling eyes, hopeful eyes. So unlike the sad eyes she had watched so intently towards the end. She could fight it no longer, her eyes slowly closed. But the image of the smile on her father's face and his hopeful eyes so bright and alive and expectant stayed on her closed eyelids as though imprinted there.

The open wound

Bandaged with love and care,

The pain, the loss, the anger,
the warmth

Father and daughter never closer

ALWAYS REMEMBERED

Visions of the past

(always with me)

Just can't and won't subside.

Lily

Jill Dawson

As soon as I saw her I recognised her. I stepped through the door, and instantly wished I hadn't. I should have gone to the hairdresser's in Romford, where Mam usually takes me, not this poky old local one, because I was bound to see people I knew, and it was bound to be embarrassing. This Saturday girl came to take my coat (a girl from our school, but I felt too shy to say hello; she was older than me), and I stared at the side of this woman's head, just to check that it definitely was her. It was. Her hair was blonde, curly, just the same really, only it occurred to me for the first time that it might be dyed. The same red pouty mouth. Lily. I ducked my eyes, to look down at the floor, at the little rings of hair that the Saturday girl would have to sweep up later, and wondered if Lily remembered me.

The girl from school came over with one of those pinnies for me to put my arms into and fastened it at my neck. While she was washing my hair I thought about Lily. She used to work in my dad's office. I don't know what she did there; I never used to think very hard about what people did at Dad's work; I just assumed they all did some kind of typing work, or looking at files of paper. Fancy her working in a hairdresser's now, that must be much more exciting, and she looked as if she was possibly the boss of it too, or nearly. I was suddenly very glad that Mam didn't come with me.

She was smoking. It must have been her break. She sat in the corner of the shop, with a mug of tea beside

31

her, talking and waving the hand with the cigarette in.
No ash fell off, so I knew she must have practised this a
lot. The girl from school was scrubbing my head with a
towel, practically taking my scalp off. I got the idea she
didn't like me, but then none of the girls in the fifth
form really do. They hate anyone who isn't in the fifth
or sixth. Lily was shouting about the way she was doing
up her kitchen and front room. She had to shout,
because the woman was under the dryer, with ten ton of
pink curlers and a hair net on, and Lily was trying to
have a conversation with her. When the girl had finished
drying my hair she sent me over to the mirror to wait,
and I knew in my bones it was going to be Lily who
'did' me.

'What's it going to be then, cut and blow dry?' She
wasn't particularly looking at me, she stared into the
mirror, holding up my wet hair between her fingers, so
that I looked funny, a bit like a Mohican. I took a deep
breath, because I was supposed to be having a cut and
blow dry, but that wasn't what I wanted at all.

'Could you cut it really short at the back and leave the
front bits longer. And could you dye it? I want all this
part blonde, and then this tuft at the front, could I have
that red?' It all came out in a huddle, the words joined
themselves together for safety, and I wasn't sure if it
made sense. For the first time Lily looked in the mirror
straight at me. I thought I saw a click of recognition in
her eyes, but then she didn't seem too sure of it, and
checked herself. Well, I was just a little girl then, about
nine or ten. I wasn't surprised that she didn't remember
me. She picked up her comb, and turned her full
attention on me.

'Blonde all over, with this bit red? Let's see what we
can do, gel, shall we?'

I closed my eyes, like I always do at the hairdresser's,
and let out my breath in a tiny sigh of relief. She was
going to do it blonde, and red, and she didn't tell me

off, or tut tut and say she couldn't do it! Now I would look totally different, exactly the way I've imagined myself looking for ages. Punky and sophisticated, not a boring freckle face with mousey hair and a fringe. I couldn't wait.

Lily combed and tugged up sections of my hair. As I watched in the mirror and saw the first curl fall on to the pinny, I thought, that's it, they've gone for ever. It's done now. And I started to relax. I love the feeling of having my hair done; it's like being small again, because then you're not allowed to do your own hair, and somebody else has to do it for you. With my eyes closed, I let my thoughts float about, and forgot about where I was. Lily smelled exactly the same, a lovely, special, party smell, but over the top of that I could smell all the strange hairdressing things, hair spray, and something dead pongy, I think it was perm solution. It was a weird combination. I started to think about when we first moved down here and about the party, where I saw Lily, four years ago.

I knew she was Dad's fancy woman the minute she walked in. The room kind of hushed. People forgot to make what they were saying sound sensible, and everything trailed off, ending with 'you know what I mean'. It was the first time I noticed how they always say 'you know what I mean' down here.

Our Mam was the first to go over to her. 'Lily! Lovely to see you, I'm glad you could make it to our little soirée!' (She giggled here.) 'Give your coat to Ralph, he'll put it in the cloakroom for you.'

The cloakroom was really the toilet. I didn't know if it was just the cloakroom for the party or if it was always going to be the cloakroom from now on, but I thought I'd better call it the cloakroom to be on the safe side.

Anyway this Lily person went to give our Dad her

coat, and I could see that Dad was sort of hanging about in the hall, as if we didn't have a front room full of people to entertain at all; and then there was silence, because the tape had finished. So our Mam shimmied over to the tape-player (it was one of those big tapes where you watch the wheels go around. Dad had borrowed it off someone at work). She shimmied because she was wearing black, shiny-stuff trousers, really wide, so that they looked like a long full dress. That was my favourite outfit. She looked beautiful, all silky and glittering, her face shining.

'This'll get you on the dance floor,' she said, putting a new tape in. It was 'Tie a yellow ribbon round the old oak tree', our Dad's favourite. Mam looked round at everyone. No one moved. Then our Hazel, who had been feeding Best Doll a whole bowl of cheese footballs, wandered out from behind Aunty Flo's bell-bottoms and began jiggling about in her pyjamas.

'Oh, isn't she a poppet?' It was the first time Lily had spoken. She came flying into the room, her face pink, and wearing this turquoise dress which was truly amazing. All crochet holes and lacy bits. I stared and stared, because underneath she looked completely bare. Mam was staring too, and Dad, who had followed Lily in. And I wanted to laugh, because Hazel isn't a poppet at all, she's dead grumpy and ugly, and no one in their right mind would call her that.

Dad clapped his hands, making me jump. 'Oh tie a yellow ribbon . . . it's been two long years, do you still want me?' he sang, getting the words wrong. He was whirling Hazel around, holding her by the ankles so that her pyjama top got ruffled up and you could see her tummy, fat and creased and rosy. She dropped Best Doll at my feet.

Mam's grey eyes were heavy lidded. She was talking to Aunty Flo, and moving her fingers up and down the stem of her glass; watching, watching. 'Put her down,

Ralph,' she said quietly to our Dad, when Hazel's
giggles finally sounded like she was being sick. Hazel
crumpled on to the floor and started screaming, so I
took Best Doll over to her, and a bowl of peanuts.

Some people had started dancing. I could feel the
carpet juddering under my feet. Mam was doing this
dance she always does; it's like a belly dance, showing
off what she calls her midriff, and making her big
earrings jingle. But she couldn't do it properly, she had
a glass of wine in her hand. She had to be careful of it
splashing. I watched her put it on the telly, then she
moved back into the middle of the people and started
wiggling her hips again.

'Having a nice time, pet?' she said once, but I
pretended not to hear her. I moved closer to Lily and
Dad, so I could study the turquoise dress better. Lily
had this long cigarette – twice the size of normal
cigarettes – and Dad was lighting it for her. I was close
enough now to notice something really weird. All her
body was one colour: a kind of peach. There were no,
well, you know, dark bits anywhere. I was secretly
disappointed. It seemed like she had something nylon,
body-coloured underneath.

Still, she was pretty, I thought, looking at her small
pointy face from underneath Dad's arm, where I was
cross-legged on the floor. She wasn't as pretty as our
Mam, of course, but her littly pursy mouth, which she
couldn't quite close over her top row of teeth, fascinated
me. It looked like the wrinkled end of a red balloon.
Dad seemed to like it too. But he caught me staring, and
he gave me A Look, so I thought I'd better take Hazel
upstairs and try and get her to go to bed.

When I came back down, our Mam had rolled out the
trolley with the party food on. Lily was dunking a piece
of carrot into cheese dip and licking her fingers the way
Mam always tells us not to. 'I love these party dips', she
was saying, 'so nice to dunk your – what are they

again?' She stood, with her little finger dangling out of her mouth smiling at the same time, looking at Mam for an answer. For some reason everyone was quiet. I could hear them all breathing. Then our Mam spoke. 'Crudités,' she said, and left the room.

Dad leapt up and changed the tape. There was a lot of bustle. Dad was filling up everyone's drink from a bottle he had, and he patted my head when he found out I'd put Hazel to bed. 'That's my best girl,' he said, looking over my head.

He didn't notice that my hair was loose for the first time. I always had to have my hair in bunches or plaits. Mam was the one who usually did it for me. But when I'd asked Mam how I should have it for the party, she just got ratty and said, 'Oh any old way.' That made me think now that she'd known Lily was going to come all along.

Mam is dead brave. We were new then, we came from up North and we talked different to everybody else. At school I tried not to talk at all. The people at the party knew our Dad better than Mam because Dad had been working at Romford first and then we had all moved down here later, to be with him. Down here they still can't pronounce my name. They call me Jiw. When they say that I didn't use to answer, but no one seems able to say Jill. That's why I never talked much.

Lily called me Jiw. 'Like a drink, Jiw?' she said, wriggling her finger at me, meaning for me to follow her into the kitchen. Mam was back in the party room, dancing again. Dad was telling a joke to someone he calls Miss Collins, who was laughing a lot. I think she is from his work, too, like Lily. I checked on what Mam and Dad were doing, then I followed Lily into the kitchen. There was only us two in there. Lily put her cigarette down, and I realised it was in a sort of holder, black plastic. Lily saw me fingering it and she clicked her tongue.

'Filthy habit. A nice gel like you wouldn't be silly enough to smoke, would she?' She was looking at me quite hard. It's bad luck to be the first to look away, so I stared back. She dropped her eyes. 'Don't you look like your dad?' she murmured, finding me a glass from the mess on the table.

When I didn't answer she went very jolly: 'I'm going to make you a snowball, how would you like that?' She started whistling. Up close she smelt lovely, like clean washing, or the soap in my knicker drawer. I sat on our high stool, swinging my legs, while her dinky fingers with the shiny nails mixed lots of lemonade with this creamy egg stuff, and plonked a sticky cherry in the top.

'There – just a small one, for a small gel, eh?'

She was smiling at me; there was lipstick on her top teeth. The dress with the holes made crisp-packet noises when she moved, and I wanted to say 'Look it's all right, I like you anyway . . .' but then our Mam came in, and I jumped off the stool so fast I hurt my toe.

'You look tired, Jill. Nearly bedtime for you.' Mam swept her eyes over the room very quickly, as if she was searching for something; only I knew she wasn't. Lily's tiny turquoise body slipped past Mam in the doorway, muttering something about missing Auld Lang Syne. Mam stood perfectly still for an instant, leaning against the half-open door. I think if someone had opened the door just then she would have fallen over. But suddenly Uncle Ron was standing there, and he coughed and took out his pipe and touched Mam's elbow. She straightened up, and us three went back into the front room.

Everyone was dancing now. Dad had put the telly on, too; all I could see were legs and swirly skirts and there was a horrible sweaty smell, like baked beans. I sat on the floor, which seemed safest. From there I looked at everyone's shoes. Mam had taken hers off. Her toes are big and looked sort of scalded, with painted red toe-nails. Lily, I noticed, had changed into elasticated party slippers, turquoise with sequins, to match her dress. Dad was next to her, in his socks (the new brown ones I got him for Christmas). Their feet were messing with each other's legs. I sipped my snowball and it was sweet like egg custard; too sweet really, I didn't like it.

Big Ben was booming on the telly, but you could hardly hear it. People had linked arms and were singing into each other's faces, and making kissy sounds. Dad kissed Mam. Mam was next to Lily now in the big circle, and at the last chime of Big Ben they were facing one another. Mam kissed Lily – quickly, as if she were shy about it – and then everyone started coming over and kissing me. They all smelt of beer, so I held my breath.

At home-time Lily found me in the cloakroom. I must have fallen asleep, because I can't remember how I got there. It was dark and fuzzy, and Lily was crouching beside me, gently tugging on my blanket. She pulled the warm, furry rug from under me, then started putting her arms into it. It turned into a fur coat. I stood up, my eyes puffy like cheese footballs, sleepy and dazed. 'Ralph –' Lily was whispering; her breath tickled my face. And then our Dad was there, picking me up as easy as if I was Best Doll, and Lily touched my cheek. My blanket had smelt of her – clean, feathery, partyish. She and Dad were whispering; Lily's eyes glittered. Then Dad carried me all the way up to bed, and that's all I can remember about that party. New Year's Eve, 1973.

It looked fantastic! I was grinning and grinning at myself in the mirror, and even Lily was smiling too, she said she had to admit I looked pretty good, even if she did say so herself.

I got down off the chair and she helped me out of the pinny, with a bit of struggling from me, because the sleeves are silly with elastic and you can't get them over your hands very easily. I saw the Saturday girl giggling behind her hand. But I didn't care. I was thinking: I don't even care what Mam says; I know she's going to be mad, but when she sees how nice I look, she'll come round. I got my coat on, paid at the desk, and I was almost out of the door before Lily said it:

'You're Ralph Waite's girl, aren't you?'

The way she said it, quietly, like she didn't want anybody else to hear, and her expression; a smile, but a worried one, with her forehead going into lines, made me realise. She'd known all along.

'Jill, isn't it?'

She pronounced it Jiw, as usual, and I nodded, my newly shorn and coloured head feeling light, unfamiliar to me. She remembered me properly. She remembered my name.

'So you still live down here? You didn't move back up North. How is he, your dad? And your mum?'

'They're very well thank you,' I said, a little stiffly.

She was blocking the doorway slightly. I felt like she didn't want me to go. Up close I could see every last detail about her, the way she had plucked her eyebrows, and the faint crease about the corners of her eyes, but she didn't look different at all, she didn't look older. If anything, she was younger than I'd thought then, quite a lot younger, although that might be because when I was little I could never tell anybody's age, and I thought anyone who was grown up must be thirty-six, at least.

'Give my love to your dad,' she said suddenly, and then paused, as if she expected me to answer. I thought it was a cheeky thing to say. I was about to run out of the shop and say nothing, since I didn't know how to reply, but then she winked at me, and I remembered the snowball she'd made me, and the cigarette in its long holder, and I couldn't help myself from smiling at her, and blushing, and saying I would.

By the time I got outside I was too busy worrying what Mam would say about my hair, and feeling wonderful and brilliant and looking at my reflection in every shop window, to think about Lily. I said to myself I would give Dad her message, if I remembered, but somehow I knew I'd almost certainly forget.

Sunni

Ravinder Randhawa

'I've never ever cried so much,' sniffed Sunni, blowing her nose on her already tear-soaked tissue as they came out into the sunlight, blinking like moles.

'Too much wickedness in this world,' Kriji's voice wobbled, sobs erupting in her throat again.

Briji took their arms and marched them off to the Chaat House. 'It's only a film,' she said. 'There'll be another one next week.'

Sunni brightened up and threw away the remaining shreds of her tissue. But Kriji still sobbed away, fumbling for the last tissue in the box she always brought with her. She had a craze for sorrow and hung on to her suffering like a leech.

Sunni and the twins lived next door to each other in Southall. They were all in the fifth form at Featherstone High School and gearing themselves up for high nervous tension with their O levels looming ahead.

But nerves were for schooldays! Weekends were for teaming up. For turning into bloodhounds or butter-flies. Flitting, sniffing from shop to shop, checking out what was new, daring and dangerous in materials, bangles and bindis. For hogging a table by the window at the Chaat House in the centre of the High Street, eyes glued to the fashion parade passing by on the pavement. Busy awarding marks and remarks, Briji and Kriji thought themselves highly suited to this demanding social task. They had rejected the cut-throat competi-tion of the fashion jungle and dressed in an unvarying uniform of dark jeans and even darker tops. Sunni was the one who tumbled in the tide of fashion, frantic to be at the front with the leaders of style.

Isn't it wonderful, thought Sunni, staring dreamily at her reflection in the window. Southall must be what Drake had set out to find, only he lost his way. Southall was the fabulous city of Samarkand, its air perfumed with the scent of a dozen spices, its shop windows sparkling with glinting arrays of jewellery, its shops stocked with sumptuous fabrics in every colour of the kaleidoscope. And its grocers' shops staying open late, spilling on to the pavement with vegetables from the four corners of the earth. You could buy mouth-watering mangoes by the golden, delicious, beautiful boxful.

It was a hot, hot summer, the glorious summer of 1976. Sunni was lazing in the back garden with a book when she heard shouting and looked up to see Briji climbing over the wall. 'Someone's been killed,' she was shouting and they were both out and racing down the street by the time she'd finished the story. Kriji and others followed them as they dashed towards the spot. They couldn't believe it. They had to go and see for themselves. Gurdip Chaggar dead, knifed to death outside the Victory pub across the road from the Odeon, home of their weekly fix of tears and techni-colour Indiana.

They joined the crowd staring at the bloodstains on the pavement. Mesmerised and breathless, Sunni heard her heart beat loudly in her ears. He had been hardly any older than they were. Her eyes saw through the red to the blade that had plunged and pierced and sliced off his life because his skin was brown. Choking laughter rose in her throat. She glanced across the road to the Odeon. If this was a film, she'd be crying.

Looking up with eyes that were hurting, she turned

and walked away. She wandered through the streets seeing a new Southall, tender and vulnerable to an old brutality. Of course, she'd always known about racism. She'd had her share of being called 'blackbird', 'Paki' and 'wog'. She'd given as good as she got in the playground. She just hadn't known it could kill.

'Paradise Lost,' she thought grimly, as she went with Briji and Kriji to the protest demonstration. It was huge, much bigger than she'd ever have imagined. Everyone was talking about the murder. Outrage ran electric through them all. When word passed through the marchers to Sunni and her friends at the back that a group of youths had been arrested, they joined the march to the police station to demand their release. Sunni and the twins joined the sit-down protest, plonking themselves down on the gritty pavement.

Cheers rang out as the captives walked out to freedom, raising their arms in victory. 'Hey, look at him,' said Sunni, pointing at the last one out as he smoothed down his Che Guevara moustache. Bursting into giggles, she dug an elbow into Briji.

'What a pseud!'

'What a poseur!'

When, at last, their O levels were behind them, they went to Omi's to celebrate over a shared mango milkshake and a samosa each. Omi's – home of the heavenly stuffed paratha, and all the other luscious goodies on display, so near, yet so far from their empty pockets. Holidays ahead and nothing to do.

Suddenly the Che Guevara moustache walked in and said 'Hi.' They looked blank, behind and around, wondering who he was talking to. He pulled up a chair and sat down next to them, ordering so much food they wondered what he'd done to be a millionaire so young.

'Hi! I'm from the youth movement. We've just got premises,' he said, 'but it's mostly blokes; well it's only blokes using it so far.' He reached down and pulled out some leaflets from his Indian shoulder bag. 'Which language would you like?'

'Goodness!' said Sunni. 'You haven't got Telagu or Konkoni,' (not that she could read either of them) 'not much of a selection is it? We'll stick to English.'

'Sorry. Printing costs are very high. But you're right, it's important not to exclude people. That's actually why I wanted to talk to you,' mouth full of saag and maki-thi-roti. 'We haven't got any women . . .'

'We don't do it for money . . .'

'Pleasure is all we want . . .'

'Most blokes can't give either . . .'

Firoz blushed and stuttered: he asked if they'd be interested in organising a women's section of the youth movement, 'As a job of course. All above board, regular paid work. The building can be allocated to you, like having women only days. How would every Tuesday suit you?'

'Only one day a week!' Sunni felt so insulted she took his plate of khardi and nan and started eating it herself. Briji and Kriji must have felt equally disgusted for they couldn't help digging in to the rest of the loot. A compromise was agreed – probably because he was still hungry. They could have the building for another day if there were enough women wanting to use it.

'Not much of a building,' they said, when he took them on a conducted tour, up and down rickety staircases, across empty rooms and past broken windows.

'We're working on it,' he said, all serious and concerned. 'Everyone has to muck in. Whatever help you want, just yell.'

And later Sunni felt rotten for having made fun of him when Briji and Kriji got hijacked by their family to a distant cousin's wedding, leaving her stranded with the first issue of *Aurat Azad*. Duplicating, collating, stapling, racing against time, fighting panic as the clock moved on, she jammed the duplicator. Firoz could have called her a cretin but he didn't. He fumbled and fiddled with it till it started again, looking triumphantly round at her with a smile bursting through the black ink on his face. Her heart flipped. 'Must be something I ate,' she told herself and tried not to think about the wonderful smile, oozing delicious danger.

The men made jokes about 'Free Women' but even they snapped up copies like the proverbial hot cakes, till Briji and Kriji started refusing.

'There won't be any left for women. How many did you print, Sunni?'

But Sunni wasn't listening. She took a deep breath and told them she wanted him.

'He's in love with his work.'

'Fall in love with a man like that and you're falling in love with disaster and pain,' intoned Kriji mournfully, puffing on her cigarette holder and blowing out imaginary rings of smoke from the sweet cigarette stuck in the end.

'I don't go for schoolgirls,' he said, putting the chairs away after a meeting one day, answering some question out of nowhere. But he went for India. Went to India, in fact, to work on a voluntary project. She knew it was silly but she felt jealous. India had taken him away from her before she'd had a chance to have him. She was restless and couldn't settle. She tried to persuade her mother to let her have a year off before her A levels.

'Don't forget you haven't got a family behind you,' said her mother, a widow. 'You have to make your way alone, you could end up ruining your life.'

But finally, after endless promises and guarantees, she agreed. Sunni wished she hadn't as soon as she started work at the community project. Each week brought a fresh crop of racist attacks: verbal and physical assaults to firebombing. She wished she was back safe in school then, except when she remembered that school wasn't safe any more either.

Then one day as she picked up the phone for the twentieth time that morning, it was him.

'Firoz speaking. There's a young girl here who's been thrown out by her in-laws. Can I send her over to you?'

She made herself sound super efficient, taking down all the details, but she couldn't stop her hand trembling as she put down the receiver. Why hadn't he rushed over to see her? Just to say hallo? She hoped it was because he was busy, as busy as she was, throwing all her mind and might into organising the New Year festivities.

1978 went out in a whirl of Giddha and folk songs and 1979 came in with coloured candles stuck in laddoos. Looking round at the happy people, Sunni patted herself on the back – then braced herself, as the Protesting Resisting Sisters Against Oppression (a.k.a. Briji and Kriji) took to the stage with poetic power to reach the parts other words never could.

Firoz and his gang were bouncers for the night. Not that she'd asked him! She'd asked someone else but they'd gone and asked him. Not that she could complain! And they did a good job of making sure no trouble-makers were let in to upset the good time. How was she to know that some of them were lingering outside to get their revenge, waiting till the others had left and Firoz was getting things ready for the van to take away?

She saw him disappear among them like a stone into water. She had never been keen on unequal odds and rushing in to help him didn't take as long as a lightning thought. And luckily the van arrived quickly – the Indians come to chase off the cavalry.

'Idiot!' Firoz shouted at her, holding his bruised stomach. 'Did I ask for your help? You could have been done over by just one of them, let alone four. Think you're Wonder Woman, do you?'

Picking up a ladle of chana, she lifted it high and ever so slowly and deliberately, tilted it over his head.

1979 was election year and Southall turned into a town under political siege. Sunni was back at school but one Saturday she bumped into Firoz handing out leaflets.

'What a pleasant surprise!' he exclaimed.

She didn't deign to reply, looking at the bunch of leaflets in his hand, but eventually allowed herself to be invited for a cuppa at Omi's. Being absent-minded, she forgot to tell him she'd arranged to meet Briji and Kriji there and, all three of them being absent-minded, they left him to pay the bill, but she remembered to take his leaflets. Sunni did think it a shame as she dumped them in the dustbin. Still, all's fair in love and politics, she thought, as she put up a poster for the Labour candidate.

The next time they met, she was giving out leaflets that weren't his.

'We *need* black MPs,' he said.

She turned and walked away. He followed and she thought she heard an apology, but couldn't be sure, so she stopped and listened and she was right, because it came again.

'Thank you,' he was saying, 'for coming to my help. It was brave of you. I'm not saying that because you're a woman, it would have been brave of anyone.'

'Thank you too,' she said. That was how it started. She couldn't believe that anyone like her could be so happy.

She bought a box of tissues and went to tell Briji and Kriji. Kriji sniffed her worries into Sainsbury's sunset pastels and waved a trembling hand as Sunni rushed off to spend an hour with Firoz before going home.

'Catch him when, how and wherever you can,' had become her motto. Firoz was a workaholic, running campaigns, going to meetings, working to solve the world's problems single-handed. Oh, but he was fun, gorgeous to look at and great to be with – when she managed to be with him alone.

'Illiterate zombie,' he said when she told him she'd never heard of half his idols, like Frantz Fanon or Malcolm X.

'Why don't you go for pop groups like everyone else?' she asked. Waiting. Wondering if he would be baited. He smiled sweetly and she wished he hadn't, as he wondered out loud about how difficult it must be to live without a brain.

She was livid and lunged at him. He evaded and attacked from behind. She hit out backwards with her elbow and heard a groan. No one believed his story about walking into a door in the dark as he and his beautiful black eye made their public appearance.

But she didn't switch from supporting Labour because of him. It was because of them. As election fever mounted, the National Front was campaigning alongside the other parties. Ealing Council said 'yes' to them: 'Yes, they could hold their meeting in the Town Hall,' when they should have said 'no'. Meetings, delegations, representations, petitions and protests fell on deaf or doubting ears.

When the morning came, it didn't seem any different from any other day, except that the streets became eerily changed, shops shuttered like rows of blind eyes. No more the hustle-bustle of everyday business; a wary expectation filled the air. As the day wore on, the empty spaces on the streets filled up with uniformed police-men, their vehicles and bodies drawing a blue square around the Town Hall, separating the crowds caught within from the crowds outside.

Sunni was caught inside, unable to meet Firoz as arranged, her stomach already churning with anxiety. The massed crowd swayed and shifted, wondering what to do next as they could no longer stick to their original plan. Then word was passed round: they would move forward and sit in front of the Town Hall.

Linking arms, Sunni, Briji and Kriji moved forward at a snail-like pace, chanting slogans, glad they could do something to show their anger at the presence of the racist fascist National Front. Sunni was looking down, watching the lines of feet trying to move in step, when Kriji's scream and Briji's hand on her arm, pulled her, stumbling and shocked, away out of danger. Briji screamed out to them to run as a line of mounted police charged into the march near them, batons sweeping into the crowd in long arcs of danger, hitting the heads and bodies of those trapped in the jammed confusion.

'We were peaceful, we were peaceful,' kept running through her head. She was shocked and dazed. The police charge had been so unexpected, so unfair.

'Here, through the park!' Briji the cool pulled them along. They flattened themselves against a wall as a lone youth ran across the grass, a mounted policeman chasing him. As the baton rose and fell on his head, Sunni ducked in pain feeling it land on her own.

'Let's move, keep moving,' said Briji, leading them away, keeping them walking, looking for a way out of the police lines.

'This is crazy,' shouted Sunni. 'They don't want us here but they won't let us get home.'

'They want to give us a beating,' said a white woman, leaning against a wall, trying to catch her breath. 'They want to give Southall what for. Quick, move!'

A police line swept down the road, truncheons at the ready, scattering people like pebbles before a flood.

They kept on the move, meandering, wandering, back-tracking, zig-zagging to avoid the police, police dogs and police horses.

'It's like being in one of those horror movies where you can't escape, no matter what you do,' said Sunni to

Briji. She took Kriji's hand. She knew her friend was too shocked to take it all in, as her longings for tragedy came true in horrible reality.

Wandering round in confused circles, they met others, picked up scraps of news and put together the jigsaws of the night. They heard of how people had been arrested, put in vans, beaten up, driven miles up the M4 and dumped. They heard how the police had rampaged through Unity House, breaking up the equipment and breaking up the people. Rumours spread of young and old arrested alike and of gangs of white youths terrorising.

But it was when she saw Firoz's face that she broke up inside. One eye had sunk in a pool of congealed blood and the rest of his face was blue-black and swollen. He wouldn't let her touch it; he wouldn't let her question him.

'Not important,' he said, 'scraps of flesh, they'll soon heal.' But she saw that his eyes would never heal, never look at the world in the same way. That was the night he left her, not physically but in his mind.

He began to talk about going. He said there was important work to be done. People had to be told about what had happened so that it wouldn't happen again.

'I don't have to know when you go,' was all she could say. She wouldn't give him the satisfaction of a clean ending. He would have to leave her behind her back, as if he was running out on her. She wouldn't make it easy, either, calling on him before going to school, sometimes bunking afternoons or whole days, holding him, pinning him with the ferocious demand of her need for him and him alone.

But she couldn't hold him. And he *did* go.

'Sunni, Sunni, Sunni,' Sunni rolled it round her tongue, backwards and forwards and over and over. Did her mother know when she named her Sunninder, that she would become Sunni? Sunni: 'left all alone'. That was what it meant in Punjabi and that was what she was now.

Briji and Kriji had opened a stall, selling their own printed fabrics. Sunni got a free sample of each, before it was even on the stall. So now she was always ahead, leader of the leaders of the followers of fashion.

Except that fashion and ogling and giggling were no longer the fun they used to be. But to her, Southall was even more precious than it had been before. Because it had been defended with blood and courage. Just because it was different didn't mean others had the right to destroy. Just because she was different didn't mean she wasn't the same too.

First Foot

Janice Galloway

It was the sun nearly w
minute I'm asleep and the
the clock. It says five to eight so I've had a good sleep.
I'm lying back congratulating myself on it when I notice
how light the room is, even through the curtains. First
sunny day of the New Year, I think. Has to be a good
sign.

I can still hear Mammy thumping about in the
living-room, putting the divan up, transforming it with
sleight of cushions into a settee again. I hold my breath
and listen, but there's still no telling what sort of mood
she's in. It's a sort of neutral thumping about. I stretch
out full, tipping the head-and-foot-board at once and
grinning at the ceiling, then sling my legs over the edge
of the bed to sit up, still listening. It does seem a wee bit
more noisy than usual right enough. Taking a bit of a
risk, I think. Maybe wake up the gorgon. And that
decides it.

I hate being in when my sister gets up. We *don't get on*,
that is to say we hate the sight of each other. I mean it
too – we've both been working on it a long time, as far
back as I can remember (and probably before that on her
side). With me, it's fear. She hates me because she thinks
everything I do is specially designed to get at her. For
example, I don't smoke/she gets through forty a day; I
wake up early/she sleeps till noon; I like peace and
quiet/she likes perpetual telly. I'm sixteen. She's thirty-
seven. I sometimes think that last bit is the crux of the

at, and my passivity. I'm really wet.
me, she knows I won't hit her back and it
orse, like she thinks I'm trying to prove I'm
an her or something. And I'm not. Irene is
ctable and vicious with it. I'm just scared sick.
n top of that, she hates mornings. She treats them
ith a fierce spite, and I'm not going to get in the way
of that, not with the day being so nice as well. I'm going
to get up and go for Joseph. Maybe go for a walk on the
shore front, down the shops, buy a magazine. Just so
long as it's out.

So I get up and I go for a wash. As soon as I turn the
taps on, Mammy shouts through for me not to use up
all the hot water, then I hear her putting the kettle on to
make me a cup of tea. I think about shouting back for
her not to bother – but I don't mind. I'm safe enough for
ten minutes or so anyway.

I put on the clothes still lying about the floor from the
night before: saves me thinking and saves me getting a
row about leaving the place a mess. I push the curtains
to one side while I'm doing up my shirt and there's the
sun. It really is glorious. One of those clear, nippy days
right at the start of the year when you think you can see
into the middle of next week and the colours are really
sharp. Wee blades of grass out the back coated with
frost and next door's washing still on the line, totally
stiff like cardboard. And there's this cartoon picture in
my head, somebody sawing the washing off the line and
bashing it with a hammer to fold it – just daft things
making me laugh and the sky pure blue and completely
cloudless.

Not much of a laughing mood .in the kitchenette,
though. Just Mammy standing at the window in her
dressing-gown and slippers. She hands the mug over
without looking at me. Then she says: 'It's you should
be making me breakfast, never mind the other way
round.'

She sometimes gets like that in the mornings, especially at holidays. Third of January already, but the haar of the New Year still hangs on round the house. She turns her back to clatter about making toast and things, muttering about ingratitude. It's the way she's woken up, and I can feel my face miserable in spite of myself. I can't stay in with this, I think. It's going to get me down and I know what happens after that. I get myself into a depression and that makes Mammy worse and then Irene gets up out of her bed like the thing from the black lagoon . . . I'm for off while I've got the chance.

So I sneak on my duffel and get my bag. Quiet. It's always important not to give the game away that I know what's coming for some reason. I try to keep my voice chirpy, but it comes out sort of flat, sort of underhand. 'I'm away out.' And while I'm drawing the door off the snib, gently so as not to wake Irene up, Mammy appears suddenly, her face hanging, at the top of the lobby.

'Where are you away to already?'

'Joe's.' I'm stalling. Then she sighs. I can hear it all the way down the lobby.

'Will you be home for your tea?'

There's a funny edge about her voice. She's really upset about something and I can see it all over her face. But I don't know what she wants me to say.

'You tell me nothing. Will you not even be in for your tea?' Her breathing is funny as well.

There's me at the other end of the lobby, feeling guilty, but I haven't a clue what I've done and I don't know how to make it better. I know she sometimes resents me going out all the time, but she just moans if I stay in. So I squirm for a minute and grab the compromise: 'Aye, okay. Okay, I'll be in for my tea,' and I shut the door fast, desperate to get out in the fresh air. I stand for a minute at the door, just breathing it in with my eyes shut.

Joe's still in his bed when I get to his place. I've to wake him up by chapping on the window and pulling faces in at him. One of the cats gets up on the window-sill when it sees me and we both climb in the window together, me laughing and calling Joe a lazy so-and-so and the cat rubbing itself like crazy off his ankles and purring for something to eat; Joe smiling away in the middle of it.

Joe's great: really good-natured. I don't think I've ever seen him lose his temper. Every other day I get him up out of bed and he just smiles and gets me something to drink and we have breakfast together. I think the house has something to do with it. He lives in this big house on the shore front and more or less on his own. His mother (a widow, like mine) stays out a lot, sometimes for days on end; and his brother's so quiet you wouldn't even know he was there half the time – he sort of tiptoes about the place. Or goes out, too. So Joe gets the run of the place; him and the three cats and the rabbit. Oh – and the tropical fish. He's been buying these tropical fish recently and he can sit and stare at them for hours. Some nights we get in a takeaway and just sit in his room watching the fish and eating the food and talking till we fall asleep. And even then, it's still me wakes him up in the morning.

Anyway, Joe's in the house by himself this morning. He fixes some grub for us and the cats, then we're out for a walk. Not that we do much or go very far: just down the rocks to look for anemones, beachcomb along the sand till we get cold. We go up the town after that and buy two cups of coffee at the Melbourne to warm our hands off them and get hysterical at the man telling us it's time we were married. He says that every time we go in there. We keep telling him we're not going out or anything, just friends, and it doesn't make any difference. I don't know whether he doesn't believe us or whether it's just a good joke for him. Joe's mother certainly doesn't think it's a joke. She's always getting on about me seeing him all the time, and wasn't it time I got myself a *proper boyfriend* and I should stop staying overnight because I'd *get a name about myself*. Joe gets really grim when she does that. It's as if they don't want us to be friends or something. Or probably don't believe that's all there is to it. Dirty minds.

We stay in there a long time, blethering. The man gives us another cup of coffee for nothing because we stay in so long and asks us what on earth we find to talk about. I couldn't tell him. It's everything and nothing. We just sort of spark each other off and we never seem to get bored with each other. This time, we're talking about the look on my mother's face this morning, but we shut up when the man comes over. Joe gets back to it after the coffee arrives, speaking and stirring with the spoon, 'She's likely just fed up,' he says. 'Just wanting you to talk to for a change. Maybe she's lonely.'

I say nothing.

'It's just not in her to ask you to stay in, either. She wants you to want to stay in.'

Now I know he's right. But I also know, and he does too, that it isn't in *me* to stay in while Irene's there. Holidays are murder.

We've finished the second cups now and Joe's up to buy a quarter of sweeties. We walk from one end of Dockhead Street to the other eating them, then back up again. Most of the shops are still closed for the New Year but it doesn't matter: we've hardly any money anyway. We're just looking. And we keep blethering the whole time. We end up back at his place with more warm coffee, staring out at the waterfront from the bay window and still talking and stroking the cats. I'm really mellow by this time, with the water and the brightness of the day and the feel of the cats' fur under our hands – full of that nice, relaxed sort of tiredness you get after a long walk. I'm happy. Then I look at my watch. My face is sliding while I'm standing up.

'I said I'd go back for my tea. I better shift.'

But he knows I'm not wanting to and he knows fine why. I keep looking out the window for a wee bit, holding on to it before I have to let go.

'I'll be away then.'

And all the time he knows perfectly well I'm dreading it, and the good time we were having isn't making it any easier. It's making it worse. I'm hoping he's going to offer to walk me back or something, then suddenly his face lights up.

'I'll come round and be your first foot! Bet that would cheer your mother up. We'll buy a bottle of that stuff she likes, take some shortbread, do the thing right . . .' And he's off into the kitchen hunting up money and biscuit tins. I'm pretty taken with the idea. Mammy likes Joe, he can make a difference to her. And the daftness of the first foot thing will make us all laugh. We'll have a present for her as well: she'll say we shouldn't have but she'll be pleased all the same. It gets better and better as I think about it.

Outside, we count up the rest of Joe's Christmas money and the dregs of my cash – enough for a half bottle of advocaat and a wee jar of cocktail cherries, for a touch of celebration. But it takes us ages to find someplace that'll sell us the drink. Bloody hell, I think, it's only advocaat. Mammy isn't too happy with drink in the house, but she does like this stuff – it doesn't count. Especially when you mix it up with lemonade. They call it a snowball and you can even give it to weans, for goodness' sake. We were giggling all the way up the road about it. I'm all warm and excited by this time, really happy inside and looking forward to springing the surprise. Me and my best friend; taking our good time and bringing it home in triumph for my mammy to share. She's always saying life doesn't give her many laughs, but when it does, she knows how to enjoy them. She's great fun when she's in the mood. And here's me bringing luck to the house with the first foot and the bottle. O aye, I'm looking forward to it.

The sight of the front door calms me down a bit, though. Irene, I think. She's been murder for the past two days and I can't afford to give her any excuse. She doesn't like me bringing folk in the house – and she doesn't like Joe. Still, no problem. We can go in the kitchenette and wait, then Mammy will come through to see what's keeping me. Fine, we can wait in there and have the drinks ready for her coming through.

I push open the door gently, shouting, 'It's me,' at the closed living-room and the two of us sneak into the kitchenette. I start looking for the glasses and Joe gets the tissue paper off the wee bottle. He's still laughing when she comes through. She just stands there in the door with her face deadly and me with my smile frozen and stuck in place.

'Where the hell have you been?'

And I just stand rooted. I'm getting dizzy.

'Where the hell were you? You said you'd be home for your tea. I had it ready for you ages ago. It's over there, cold and dry as dust. And you'll bloodywell eat it if it chokes ye. Good money wasted.'

Her face is really bitter. She's noticed Joe and flinches a bit with being so angry in front of him, but that doesn't stop it. And the violence of it knocks the stuffing out of me and everything I wanted to say.

Joe fumbles in: 'She's been at my place Mrs Galloway, we've been –'

But she's too mad to listen. She's shouting: 'Well take her back there then. On ye go. Never want to be in here anyway; quick as ye can get out in the mornings. On ye go. Get out of my sight. Away with your friends: let them feed ye.' Her whole body is trembling.

I'm trapped with my own speechlessness. I'm wanting to yell, to make her see. I want her to notice the bottle we've brought. And she does see it, but only with her eyes. It still doesn't mean anything to her – just a bottle on the table and a jar of daft cherries. I want her to really see it, recognise it for what I mean it to be – some kind of a token and some sort of prayer it's impossible to speak out loud in this damned house. I want her to see all that at once and stop, take it and pour it out and drink hopefully to the New Year; to accept it. Accept *me*. It's not just a bloody drink I've brought her – I'm trying to tell her I love her. But I know she's too blind and too angry. And I know who's done the blinding. Irene.

I want to scream, but I know I won't. I never do. Instead, I just burn with guilt, shame and self-disgust.

I'd been stupid. I should have known what my sister could do when my back was turned. Then her voice floats in, sickly sweet, from the living-room. 'Don't upset yourself with her, Mammy. Just come away through. Leave her with her "friend".' And my mother just turns her heel and goes.

Me and Joe just stand in the kitchenette. He doesn't speak, he's waiting, afraid for what I might do. Then I feel the tears starting down my face and I run to hide in the bedroom, just stand and stare at the frozen washing still on the line outside. My jaw hurts with biting it down: *Mammy, don't listen to her, help me to find the words for once.* But it goes on hurting and I know I won't say it. I know I won't ever say it.

Staring, cursing our weakness, I make up my mind, *Let her win.*

I start gathering my things together.

Once Upon a Time

Mary Hooper

*I stand, poised and beautiful, before the full-length mirror.
The lights studded all round its frame, Hollywood-style, light
up my white Jasper Conran dress and make it look almost
luminous. I turn this way and that, flicking my hair from my
shoulders. Thank God I'd gone to Sassoon's to have it
streaked. No one understands my hair the way they do . . .*

'Elizabeth!' Mum says, coming into the hall. 'You're
never going out in that white thing. It's too tight to
walk in!'   .

'No it isn't,' I say, leaving the mirror and walking up
and down the hall to prove it.

She shakes her head. 'It's a strange-looking thing.
Where did you get it from, anyway?'

'What?' I pretend to be looking round for my bag.
'Now, I must rush,' I say, in a rushy way.

'I said, where did you get it?'

'In town. The . . . er . . . Oxfam shop,' I say,
coughing on the last two words and hoping she won't
pick them up.

'The Oxfam shop?' From the horror in her voice I
might as well have said I'd bought it from a leprosy
camp.

'Yes. Now, I must go,' I say. 'Back at twelve, right?'

'Back at *eleven*. And, Elizabeth, just a minute. What's
happened to your hair?'

I brighten up. 'Can you actually see any difference,
then?'

'Certainly I can. What on earth have you done to it?'

I bend my head in front of the mirror. It's on a stand and it's got two clothes brushes dangling in front of it so it's pretty difficult to see anything at all. 'I used this kit. You pull bits of hair through a polythene bag.'

Mum looks confused. 'But whatever *for*?'

'To streak it blonde. I can't see much difference, myself.'

'Well, I can. It's all orange at the ends.'

'Thanks a bundle, Mum.'

'I suppose it's all for some boy or other.'

'I must go,' I say hurriedly. 'See you later.'

I turn the corner and pull into the club car park with a screech of brakes. A few guys look at my BMW admiringly and then notice me and do a double-take – probably wondering how I handle such a powerful car. I smile lazily; fast cars and me grew up together. I slide across the red leather seat, get out and slam the door, then airily toss the keys to one of the lackeys outside the club so that they can park it for me . . .

'You never came on that bike, Liz!' Emma says.

'What?'

She sighs. 'Day-dreaming again! You were in a trance just now. Sometimes I wonder how you ever find your way here. I said, did you ride that bike all the way?'

I nod.

'In that dress? It's a wonder you didn't split it.' She looks at me curiously. 'What are you doing now?'

'Pushing my bike into the hedge,' I say, 'so it won't get pinched.'

'I shouldn't think anyone would bother to pinch it. It's not exactly the most stylish bike in the world, is it? I reckon you've had it since primary school.'

I ignore her and nod towards the low red building that passes as a disco, youth club, Mothers' Union, playgroup and you-name-it in our town. 'Have you been in, yet?'

She nods. 'Yes. And before you ask, Alan Pargiter *is* there.'

'Alan who?' I say, but I'm grinning like a Cheshire cat.

We push open the doors and a girl scurries to take our jackets. The man on the door bows deeply. 'How nice to see you,' he simpers. 'Usual table?' I nod dismissively and sweep in. People stop dancing, stop talking, almost stop breathing at my entrance. 'It's her, it's really her!' someone cries in an awe-struck voice.

The lights are low, the carpets thick, the decor luxuriously understated. I sink onto a small gold chair and let the music surround me in a smooth bank of sound . . .

'Hey!' Emma is shaking my arm. 'I said, shall we sit near the stage or near the loo?'

'Near the stage.'

'Bit close to the speakers,' she says. 'I had earache last time. It's when they do that high-pitched whistle.'

'In between the two, then.'

We pick our way through little knots of people standing about shouting at each other and make our way to two hard wooden chairs by the window. The hall smells a bit funny: a bit like a jumble sale and a bit like a cubs' Sausage 'n' Bean Bake, which it was the venue for the night before.

Someone has pinned two balloons on to the DJ's table, but apart from that it is just the same: wooden chairs and benches, dusty floor, green curtains with holes in them and notices which say: 'Dustbin Collection Days' and 'What to do if there's a Sewage Workers' Strike'. I sit down and let out a sigh.

'What's up with you?' Emma asks.

'This place – everything about it,' I say gloomily.

'It's somewhere to go. It's a disco, isn't it – *and* Alan

Pargiter's here. What more could you want?'

'Lots more.'

'You're always dreaming, that's your trouble.'

'I've got to,' I say, 'I've got to pretend or I can't be bothered to do anything. Take tonight, for instance: Alan Pargiter won't come near me, I know he won't. He'll look at me, he might even smile at me, but he'll stay with his mates and I'll stay with you and that'll be it until the next disco.'

'So?'

'So I've got to make up something to keep me going until then. I'm going to pretend to myself that he comes up to me and sweeps me off to dance and then takes me home in his car.'

·Emma rolls her eyes. 'He hasn't got a car. Anyway, what would you do with your bike, pull it along behind?'

We get up to dance. The dance-floor is a sunken square of coloured lights which flicker on and off in time to the music. Bathed in a sea of colour and sound, I begin to move to the beat.

'Wow!' Emma says admiringly. 'If only I could dance like you.'

She stands back to give me more room and suddenly there is a circle of admirers all round me, swaying and clapping me on, yelling and screaming.

'Fantastic!' I hear someone shout. 'She knocks spots off everyone else.'

'I hear they wanted her to star in a Hollywood musical but she had too many other film parts,' someone else says . . .

'D'you think our handbags will be all right under the table?' Emma says. She screws up her nose, 'Why are you dancing all funny?'

'*Am* I?'

'You're flinging yourself all over the place. People are

looking at you.'

'Sorry.' I go back to dancing normally, then look over Emma's shoulder for Alan. Finding him, I point myself in his direction and stay staring at him.

'Now you're dancing all stiffly. Like a puppet.'

'I'm watching Alan,' I explain, 'so I've got to stay in the same place.'

'What's he look like?'

'Wonderful.' As if he's ever looked anything else in all the months since I first saw him. Four months now: ever since the Valentine's Disco.

Emma and I have a couple of dances and sit down again.

'I think I'll go and have a word with Ray Millar,' she says after a moment, 'let him know I'm available. Will you be all right here on your own?'

' 'Course I will,' I say. Ray Millar is Emma's ex and she's been letting him know she's available almost every day since they split up.

She goes off and I sit back in my seat, well aware of the admiring glances but trying not to attract attention. It's going to get too boring if everyone starts coming up with autograph books.

'Excuse me,' someone says, and I look disdainfully at the guy standing there.

'Yes?' I reply wearily. 'I've come here incognito, you know. I was hoping to have a quiet evening.'

'Of course. Of course,' he says humbly. 'I just wondered if you'd be interested in a new film part.'

'Send the script to my agent,' I snap. 'I really can't discuss it here.'

'Of course not. Thank you for letting me speak.'

He melts away into the crowd and I look round for the incredibly handsome star who is my escort tonight. Ah, here he is, pushing his way through the crowd . . .

'Hi!' Alan Pargiter says.

I make a strangled noise.

'You okay? You look a bit . . . as if you weren't quite with us.'

'I was . . . er . . . day-dreaming,' I say.

He grins. 'Yeah. I do it myself.'

I pinch myself but he doesn't disappear. *It isn't a day-dream*!

'I saw your mate go off so I thought I'd come over. I've been wanting to come and chat for a while.'

'You have?' I say disbelievingly.

He nods, hesitates. 'So, shall we have a dance?'

I get up, he puts his arms round me and the music swells, the lights go glittery and the hard wooden chairs turn into little gold ones.

Well, actually, they didn't – but Alan Pargiter *was* dancing with me and a girl can't have everything, can she?

Dreaming
Sandra A. Agard

She bolted upright in the bed and tried to calm herself. She felt hot and her heart was racing. She could hardly breathe. Her eyes tried to focus on something familiar and she fought a surge of panic as nothing fell into place. She stifled a burning desire to scream, then spied Pauline, her old rag doll, sitting limply on the window sill. She sighed with relief as her room began to take shape.

There were the books resting unopened on the desk; as always, homework undone. A picture of Miss Collins, her English teacher, loomed menacingly before her. She dismissed it hurriedly from her mind. On the armchair her clothes were flung carelessly. Her mother would give her another lecture: 'For a young lady, you are a disgrace, Donna.' She would go on and on. Donna dismissed that scene from her mind as well.

What had scared her so much? Almost immediately she remembered the dream, or rather the nightmare it had become. She tried to think of other things but the dream remained battling for supremacy in her thoughts, so for a while she gave in and settled back underneath the quilt and let the dream that had been invading her sleep for the last two weeks take over.

She was standing in a room that seemed vaguely familiar but she had no recollection of ever having been there. A yellow lamp bathed everything in its light, giving a friendly expression. There were four chairs around a table laid for a meal with four place settings. In a corner of the room, there was a very old fashioned television set. There was also a small coffee table on which there was a pack of cards and a box of dominoes. As she looked round, her eyes came to rest on the flower-patterned walls and the pictures that hung on them.

She recognised the countryside as being from her mother's home in the Caribbean. Yes, her mother would often speak of the deep green hilltops, the clear running water, the birds and the insects that lived amongst the trees and grasslands, the burning of the canefields, and a land that bore fruit ready to eat. The scenes of the beach were also from her mother's home. They pulled her into their sparkling world – sparkling with the setting sun disappearing into the misty horizon.

As she looked more deeply into one of the pictures, Donna could feel the warmth of the fading sun and hear the sea gently caressing the shore line. She felt herself stepping into the picture. Her feet sank into the golden warm sands. She left the room with its sense of vague familiarity for a world that embraced and welcomed her. Palm trees surrounding the beach seemed to shelter it from an outside world. The songs of unseen birds filled the air. The smells of ripe fruit hung on the breeze. Gazing happily at the setting sun, she rejoiced in the rich reds, deep golds and brilliant purples that were being painted in the sky, and wished she could stay in this beautiful and peaceful world for ever.

But the new-found happiness was shattered by the sound of something breaking behind her – from the room she had left. She turned back. The room appeared to be as she'd left it, but on a closer look she saw it was not. It was filled with the shadowy forms of figures moving to and fro; she was sure she had been alone.

Donna called out to the figures but they did not hear her. So she began to run towards the room, away from the beach with its palm trees, sunset and peace. She couldn't make out the faces of the figures, except one – her own. This made her run faster but the sand that had at first been so welcoming now hindered her. Her feet sank deeper into its depths and the more she struggled, the harder it became. She couldn't reach the edge of the picture and get back to the room. She fell exhausted into the sand, her unheard screams of frustration ringing in her head.

Donna had not told anyone about this strange dream, not her mother or even Sharon or Christine. She knew her mother was beginning to worry, seeing her daughter looking so tired every morning. But when her mother asked her if everything was all right, she would say, 'Really Mum, I'm fine. Everything's okay now.'

She knew her mother was thinking about the running battles with the teachers that had marred Donna's first weeks at the new school, when she had answered every question with her fists and insults. She recalled her very first encounter with the formidable Miss Collins. Donna had refused to answer a question and had taken out a magazine and begun to read it. She learned later that this defiant action was thought very brave indeed, and had won her great admiration. She had refused to co-operate with anyone and had picked fights with anyone who dared come near her. But recently she had made friends. Sharon and Christine had ignored her fighting ways and insults and taken as their companion the girl who had just lost her father.

Could she tell them about the dream? She had to tell someone. Maybe I'll tell Mum in the morning, she thought. But she decided against it at once. Mum had enough on her plate, she decided, I'll have to sort this out myself. I need a drink, she thought. She got out of bed and went downstairs to the kitchen where her cat, Mr Tibbs, welcomed her unexpected attention in the middle of the night. She was beginning to feel ashamed of her persistent dream. After all, she was fifteen. Sharon would laugh at her anyway she realised, and put it down to some adolescent fantasy. Sharon had just started the new psychology course at school! Maybe Chris might have an answer. It must mean something, there must be a logical explanation. Oh no, I'm starting to sound like Sharon, she thought, and shivered and laughed at the prospect as she climbed the stairs.

What's the time? She looked at the alarm clock. Only a quarter to three. I could always do that English homework, that would please old Miss Collins. But she quickly decided against it. She could just as easily do it on the bus tomorrow. What about that book? Now where did I put it? She got up and searched for the book, finding it under a pile of clothes she had flung in a corner. Secretly she vowed to tidy up the room soon. She took the book back to bed and, after glancing once more at the clock, she made herself comfortable, opened up the book and started to read.

The next thing she knew, her young brother, Michael, was standing over her, urging her to get up.

'Get lost,' she said, beneath sleepy eyes.

'Mum said you have to get up now . . . and that you're getting lazy.'

Donna flung the pillow at him and he ran out, laughing. Why did she have to have a brother so young? she thought for the thousandth time.

She looked at the clock. It was nearly eight. The book lay on the floor where she'd dropped it. She yawned widely. She felt exhausted, as if she'd been jogging. Immediately the dream came back to her.

'Do you plan to stay in that bed all day, young lady?' her mother's voice called from the door.

When Donna didn't move, her mother came closer. 'Donna, what's the matter with you?' Her voice had lost its earlier harshness. 'You've not been yourself lately, so tired in the mornings. Aren't you sleeping well? Are you having trouble at school again? I thought you were happy now.'

'Everything's fine, Mum, I'm just a little tired, that's all.'

'I know it's been hard . . . the change and everything . . .' her mother's voice seemed to falter, 'but we all went through it. Jobs were so hard to find in Marshfields. When this job came up in Lincoln General, I couldn't pass it by . . .'

'I know, Mum . . .'

'Then what is it? Everything's been difficult since your father departed.'

'Yes, I know. Everything's okay. Don't worry.'

'Well, if you're sure . . . you'd better get up or you'll be late for school again.'

Donna did not move. 'Mum,' she began, 'do you ever think of Home?'

'Home? . . . Marshfields, yes . . .'

'No . . . Back Home.'

'Back Home . . .?' She thought for a while and then said, 'Sometimes . . .'

'Why have you never been back?'

'Too busy bringing up four disgusting children, for a start,' she said with a short laugh.

'Come on, Mum, it's not that bad!'

'That's what you think!'

And as they both laughed, Donna thought, Why not tell her now? 'Mum,' she began, 'I've been having . . .'

'Mum, where's my grey shirt?' called a voice from the door.

Her mother turned towards the voice. 'Paul have you looked where you lot always leave your things, in that pile on the floor of your room? You kids drive me crazy at times . . . Now, Donna, what were you saying?'

'Oh, it's nothing.'

'Then may I suggest you get up and get ready for

school or have you got a sore back like your sister . . .
Angela! You'd better get out of that bed before I have to
come and tend to you . . .' She left the room.

She wouldn't have believed me anyway, thought
Donna. I'm beginning not to believe myself. She looked
at the clock, let out a yell and leapt out of bed.

School passed with its usual routine. Donna had
forgotten to do her homework on the bus so Miss
Collins gave her a detention.

'What's up with you lately?' asked Christine during
the break.

'What do you mean?' asked Donna.

'Well, you've been acting a little strange recently . . .
Want to talk about it?'

'You sound like the good Dr Sharon Jarvis.' They
both laughed.

'Seriously though, what's wrong?'

'Just a few sleepless nights, nothing I can't handle.'

'Look Donna, you're falling asleep in class.'

'I don't do I? I didn't know I was that bad.'

'Are you in any trouble?'

'No . . . Don't worry, I'm not going to turn into that
strange thing that took over when I first came to
Grayston High.'

'Well, you better try to catch up on all that
homework.'

'Don't worry, I plan to do it all tonight.' Donna was
thinking quickly. She decided to tell Christine. 'Chris
. . .' she began.

'Yeah . . .'

'Do you ever have dreams?'

'Sure . . . doesn't everyone?'

'But what do you dream about?'

'Hmm . . . I don't ever remember. Want a sweet?'

'No thanks. You never remember any of your
dreams?'

'Nope. Can't be very important! Why?'

'Well, you see I . . .'

'Do you two young ladies plan to sit here all day?' came a voice from behind them. It was Miss Collins. 'I would think that you, Donna Francis, are in enough trouble already without being late for Mr Thomas' maths lesson.'

The two girls gathered their books, mumbling their apologies, and fled from Miss Collins' disapproving looks.

'What were you about to tell me before old fish-face butted in?'

'Oh, nothing. Just a silly dream I had last night. Come on, I can't bear to get another stretch of detention.'

That night Donna was standing in the yellow room, this time facing the picture of the deep green hilltops. She heard the running water and the birds and insects that lived amongst the grasslands, and once more she was pulled into the midst of the picture. The sun was just rising in a faintly red sky. Early morning dew passed through her bare feet as she walked over the grasslands, enjoying the freshness and peace all around her. The aroma of burning cane lingered on the air. Suddenly she heard something breaking behind her, in the yellow room. She turned and tried to get back, but the room seemed to pull away from her desperate grasp. The shadowy forms were there pulling at the figure that had her face. She sank exhausted into the green foliage and never reached the edge of the picture.

She woke up, heart racing, struggling for breath, her throat dry and parched. She had to tell someone about this dream. I'll tell Sharon tomorrow, she'll have some kind of explanation, she decided. And, having made up her mind, she went downstairs to get her nightly drink of water and to stroke the now expectant Mr Tibbs.

The next day, Sharon was not at school. The psychology class had gone out for the day to a lecture on – what else? – psychology. Just her luck. Now who was she going to tell? Christine was in the library. She spent every minute she could there, studying for her mocks. Donna knew she ought to be there too. She spent a miserable day, especially as it ended with another spell of detention. 'Just to keep you on your toes,' Miss Collins had said with a gleam in her eyes.

Donna arrived home to find her mother reading a letter.
'Mum!' called Donna.
'Oh Donna, I didn't hear you come in,' said her mother, putting down the letter. 'You're looking very tired. Are you sure you're sleeping properly?'
'Sure,' said Donna, too confidently.
'Then how come for the past couple of nights you've been walking around this house?'
Mum misses nothing, thought Donna. For a few minutes she stared at the woman who had borne all the responsibility when Dad had died after his illness. She had nursed and cared for him at home and, when he went into hospital for the final time, she had watched over him, and yet always seemed to be there for them too. And what a jerk she had been herself, throwing tantrums. Donna had hated leaving Marshfields, her friends, the memories. But Mum must have had it worse, she thought.
Donna bent and gave her mother a kiss on the cheek.
'What's that for?' asked her mother in a surprised voice.
'Does there have to be a reason to kiss my own mother?'
'In your case, yes. You have no more pocket money to get this week, young lady.'
'Mum, you're such a sceptic. I don't want anything.'
'With children like you all, suspicion comes with

practice.'

Donna decided to take the plunge. 'Mum, do you ever dream?' she asked quietly.

'What kind of question is that? Everyone has dreams. Is that why you're having these restless nights – bad dreams?'

Donna nodded.

'Come on, let's sit by the window.' They moved towards the settee. 'Now, tell me all about these dreams,' urged her mother, gently.

Donna poured it all out: the yellow room with its flowered wallpaper, the table laid for a meal, the TV, the small coffee table with the pack of cards and the dominoes, and the pictures of the beach and the countryside. How it all seemed so real that she could step into them and become part of them and how happy it made her feel. Then the panic and fear which took over when she heard the sound of something breaking, crashing into her joy, and finally the frustration when she couldn't return and the strange people trying to restrain her.

Her mother listened patiently. She didn't speak immediately after Donna had finished and, when she did, her voice sounded different.

'There was a room like that a long time ago . . . You were very young.'

I'd *known* the room, that's why it was familiar to me, thought Donna. She wanted to ask questions but realised that her mother would move at her own pace, so she waited in tense anticipation.

'It was the dining-room,' continued her mother. 'We would entertain our friends at our famous Saturday cook-ups . . . The pictures of Home were everywhere, but you loved best the two you described in your dream. I'd tell you stories about the places in the pictures. You used to beg me to tell you stories every minute of the day.' She smiled at the memory. 'But who'd have thought you'd have remembered that night!'

'What night? What happened?' said Donna impatiently.

'It was the usual Saturday cook-up, your Uncle John and Aunt Juliette had come round. I was telling you a story. Your father and your uncle and aunt were playing a noisy game of dominoes, or was it cards? I can't remember.'

Donna wished she could hurry her mother up. It was now completely dark and, except for a street lamp that cast the room in a hazy silvery light, they sat in the semi-darkness, wrapped in the story of the past.

'That night started off so ordinary . . .' she paused, and Donna felt her body shudder. 'There was a knock at the front door. They were too busy with their game, so I went to see who could be calling that late in the evening . . . It was the postman. I knew at once it was bad news. He handed me a telegram – a telegram from Home. I couldn't open it. Your father did.

'My mother had died suddenly. I fainted, and as I fell I hit the table, spilling some of the plates. You tried to come to me but someone took you out of the room. You were crying and screaming, your father told me later. It was a very sad evening.'

Silence filled the room. They sat in the darkness, each with their thoughts.

'How old was I?' asked Donna.

'Five.'

'How come I remember all that now?'

'Who knows! Maybe we should ask Sharon as the budding psychologist in our midst!' They both laughed, welcoming the light relief.

'Is that why you never went back?' asked Donna.

'Maybe that's part of the reason . . . then there was your father's illness . . . there never seemed to be enough time . . . And then there was *no* more time left for him . . .' she added sadly. 'Now could be the time,' she said, almost to herself.

'Do you think that's what the dreams *mean*, Mum?' Donna almost shouted. 'The way they pull me in?'

'I don't know . . . Who can really understand the tricks of the mind?'

'But Mum, they're all so *real*, the colours, the smells, the sounds, everything.'

'Well, you always did have a vivid imagination, my girl, and lots of energy. I wish you'd put some of it into tidying up your room or doing your homework. What's the time?'

'Oh Mum, you always spoil things. I think you should tell me a story now. You haven't done that for ages.'

'Girl, there's a time and a place for everything. Right now, I'd like to find out why this house is so quiet. What's the time?'

'Nearly seven.'

'This letter is from Home . . . Yes, I think it's about time we went.'

'You mean Go Home?'

'Yes, but don't get excited yet, it won't be tomorrow. And it depends on things like doing one's homework on time, and no detentions!' Her mother eyed her sharply.

'Who told you about the detentions?'

'Never mind who told me. Less of them or, better still, none at all, young lady!'

'I bet it's that Michael. I'll get even with him!'

'You've got away with a lot lately.'

'Mum . . . do you miss Dad?'

'Do *you*?'

'Of course!'

'Then do you need to ask?'

'No. I'm sorry. It was a silly question.'

'You seem to be growing up, my girl! Now, why's it so quiet? Go and see what Michael's doing. Angela!

Paul!' she shouted. 'I hope it's homework that's keeping you so quiet!'

Donna knew that the unique atmosphere she'd shared with her mother was over, for the moment anyway. But as her mother walked out, she knew that she could persuade her to tell her a story again. And with that thought, she got up to tackle the day's homework.

That night she dreamt she was running along a golden beach where the palm trees seemed to bow down towards her, and then down green-covered hills with the sun caressing her gently. The sky was aglow with reds, golds, purples and blues. It was so beautiful and so real and this time there was no interruption from the room. Her companions were not only birds and insects, but people – people she did not know, but who seemed familiar and welcomed her Home.

She woke up feeling fresh and energetic in contrast to the grey dullness she could see through the window. As always, she was greeted by Michael, but this morning she didn't mind.

'Hey, Donna, what've you been up to?' he asked from the window-sill.

'Hmm . . . what?' Donna stammered.

'Well, why's Pauline covered in sand?'

'What are you talking about?' she yawned.

'There's sand all over the floor. I'm going to tell Mum,' and he ran out of the room.

Donna got up and walked over to her doll that leaned against the window. Something was prickling her bare feet. When she looked down, there were grains of sand and small tufts of grass. Donna stared at the pieces from her dream and pinched herself to make sure she was awake.

'Donna!' her mother called from the door. 'Are you going to school or are you going to stand there with Pauline all day?'

'Mum . . .' began Donna.

'Yes.'

'Mum, where are the pictures now?'

'In the suitcase in the spare room. You're not looking at them now, you're supposed to be getting ready for school.'

'Will you tell me a story tonight?'

'Maybe . . . I think your head is full of stories and dreams already. What are you staring at?'

'Mum . . . There's . . .'

'Mum, where are my socks?' a voice called from the landing.

'Why are you asking me? Why don't you children ever pay attention to what you're doing? Now, what were you saying, Donna?'

'Oh . . . nothing,' said Donna. It had to be her imagination.

'Well, get a move on, then! Angela, I hope you're up!' She left the room.

Donna looked once more at the evidence of her dream. I've a fantastic imagination, she thought. She put on her bathrobe, picked up a towel and walked slowly out of the room, wondering . . .

Gentle Persuasion
Esther Bloom

'The Leek Soup looks like bile.'

'Oh *Rachel*! Sh!' says Judy, hitting her arm. 'Can't take you anywhere!'

Judy finds a vacant table and methodically empties their trays on to it. She starts to eat, methodically.

'I'm going to a party on Saturday,' says Rachel.

'Oh yeah, whose?'

'I dunno, they're these blokes who Gina knows. They asked her to bring as many girlfriends as possible, to make up the numbers. Lend me your blue dress?'

'My brand new dress? You've got to be kidding!' shrills Judy. All the female members of their family have eardrum-piercing voices when they're excited.

'Oh, go on, I'll wash it and everything,' wheedles Rachel in her little-girl voice, jutting out her bottom lip. They both know Judy is going to give in, but she will enjoy the sight of Rachel grovelling for as long as possible. They eat. Rachel savours every mouthful. Judy shovels it in, fast and furious.

'Did I tell you Josephine's finished with her boy-friend?' Judy launches in.

'No.'

'Didn't take her long to find someone else. She met him on the tube, this new one; just sat down next to her and started chatting. He's quite nice, really.'

'If he's quite nice, what's he doing with her?' Rachel tosses her long heavy hair. It feels soft and luxurious on her back and shoulder blades.

Judy chuckles, and shrugs, 'I dunno. She's got something. Sex, I suppose.'

'But he can't *fancy* her. Those teeth! Anyway you've just side-stepped the issue.' The man at the next table is openly listening to their conversation. This makes Rachel speak louder and spice up what she says.

'What issue?'

'The dress!'

'Oh, that.'

'I did make the quiche last week when I got to your flat before you came home. I must be the only person in the world who gets invited to dinner and then has to cook it herself!'

Judy laughs. She is not going to make it too easy for Rachel.

Judy is tidily arranging vegetables on her fork. Rachel has poured the salt on to the wooden table, and has made sand dunes in it with her knife. Judy cares what people think, Rachel doesn't. Judy is practical. She is very neat and thinks everyone else should be too. Once, when Rachel was at university, Judy went to stay with her and tidied up her flat. Rachel could not find her notes; heavy objects were thrown. It was several days before Judy was forgiven.

'You haven't got any shoes to wear with it.'

'My white ones would look all right.'

'Maybe I want to wear it on Saturday.'

'Why, where're you going?'

'Nowhere.'

'Well then. Oh *please*, Jude!'

'Hmm, I'll think about it.' Judy frowns. This will cause terrible lines on her face. A boy once told Rachel that she was hands down prettier than her sister. Far from being pleased, she felt wracked with hurt on Judy's behalf.

Rachel sips her coffee. 'We went to see that fringe play, the one about Montgomery Clift.'

'Who's he?'

'Don't you know? He was this Hollywood film star of the fifties. He was gay and he topped himself.'

'Sounds lovely,' says Judy drily. 'Was it good?'

'Well, I think it was trying to be deep. Anyway, Adam Ant was in the audience, and I *leaned* on him!'

'Who?'

'Adam Ant, he used to be a pop star years ago. I was trying to be nonchalant and not stare, but he was so unobtrusive, in the interval I found I was practically *standing* on him!'

'Well, what was he like?'

'I don't know, I couldn't look at him properly, I was too embarrassed.' Rachel looks at Judy's plate. 'Are you going to finish that?' she says, her fork poised. Judy's been so busy cramming her face she's had to stop and surreptitiously undo the button of her jeans. Rachel always has more room for anything containing chocolate.

Judy shakes her head. 'You can have it if you like. You're much too thin and peaky.' She raises her voice to a stage whisper – 'Are your periods okay?'

'For God's sake!' Rachel tosses her fork on to her plate in disgust, causing a large blob of cream to ricochet on to the man at the next table. Rachel glowers at him, he cowers away from her.

'Shh,' says Judy severely.

Searching for a way of soothing Rachel, she brings the conversation back to the subject of clothes.

'You know that cloth I bought? The blue with the pink squiggly bits?'

'Fuchsia,' interrupts Rachel, sulkily.

'Well, I thought of making it into a two-piece, skirt and top. I got a new pattern from *Vogue*.' Judy went to fashion college. Her hands are large and dependable. She also spent two years designing knitting patterns. Well, somebody has to.

'Are you going to let me borrow it?'

Judy shrugs. She'll spin it out just a little bit longer.

'Oh, go on!'

'Rachel! I'm still thinking about it!'

But they know the battle is nearly over.

'I got a pair of white ski pants with Grandma's birthday money,' Rachel keeps the conversation on clothes. 'The day after, Mummy went out and brought me three pairs of white panties 'cos she could see my red ones underneath.'

'She spoils you, you know.'

'I know. But she'd spoil everyone if she could.'

'Don't let her do too much around the house.'

'I do help her as much as I can, but I can't do Daddy's share as well!'

'He's had a hard time of it! And he works very hard.'

'I didn't say he didn't,' says Rachel.

'Oh, you think you're so clever!' attacks Judy.

'I don't,' says Rachel. But she knows Judy thinks she's clever. And she is. That makes it worse. She must now play her trump card.

She bows her head, her face crumpling. 'I don't mean to be a burden on them,' she cries. 'I wish I had enough money to repay them. I didn't have a breakdown on purpose.'

'Shh! All right, all right, I know!'

Rachel sniffs. She feels bad about using this weapon. She makes a big thing about mopping up her tears. Judy wipes her nose for her.

'May I borrow it?' she weeps.

'I suppose so,' sighs Judy.

Changes
Millie Murray

'Mum, you don't understand,' I cried. I stood facing her back, pleading with her to see my point. Her broad hands were immersed in soap suds. She was oblivious, it seemed, to what I was saying.

'Me nar know why yu want fi go ah 'olland fe stay overnight. Me know definitely dat yu fadda will not understand. Me know how yu young people stay.' She began to scrub at the frying pan furiously, putting all her energy into it.

I sighed and leaned back against the fridge. The cool metal soothed my anger. 'Oh Mum, it's not like that at all, it's really just a disco. Music, dancing, and all the girls sleep in one room,' I said softly.

Mum span round like a whirlwind and stalked towards me, face contorted, fingers pointing accusingly. 'Disco! Music! All de gal dem sleep inna one room! Yu really tink sey me a fool, ee? What happen when yu come back wid belly and can't finish college? Move yurself!'

Mum's shoulders sagged, as though all her energy had been spent. She turned and went back to the sink. Her head slightly cocked, she said over her shoulder, 'When I was young, I would go ah dance, and partee and stay a lickle while and come home. De gal dem dat stay out all night would come home too, but wid belly. Dat's all me know.' She emptied the bowl of suds and dried her hands on the tea towel. Her head hung and her shoulders hunched. I felt terrible and took a few steps towards her. Mum looked up and held out her arms to me. I threw myself into them, loving the feel of her bosom against my head. Her strong arms were a protection, and would ward off any harm. My dad, I hoped.

I went upstairs to my bedroom and sat on the window-ledge, the place where I make all my decisions, and tried to work out why my mum had taken the idea of my going to Amsterdam so badly. Perhaps it was because Steve had arranged it and they don't know him. Perhaps it was because it was an overnight trip and there would be boys, but if I had told her it would be all girls, would she have reacted differently? I decided I had better get to work on Dad as soon as possible before Mum started to give him her version of things. I brushed my hair, straightened my clothes and sat on the end of the bed. Closing my eyes I breathed in deeply, breathed out and counted from ten backwards, '. . . Five, four, three, two, one.' I waited for a surge of confidence to rise from deep within me. Nothing. Instead I felt panic. I leaned across to the bedside table and picked up the book that my best friend Sandra had lent me. *How to be Successful in Ten Easy Steps*. I turned to page forty-eight and the chapter entitled, 'When Needing More Confidence'. Repeating a sentence over and over again to yourself, it said, will eventually make it real. I began to pace the room. 'I will tell my dad about Holland. I will tell my dad about Holland. I will tell my dad . . .' I was still saying this to myself as I entered the living-room.

Dad was reading the paper in his reclining chair. He looked at me over his gold-rimmed glasses and turned back to his paper. Not encouraging. On the table beside him was a brandy glass with just a little drop of brandy in it. His silver-plated pen lay on top of his pools coupon, beside his Bible. This was obviously not the right time to approach him. Dad went to great lengths to work out his pools, which left him slightly unstable, and to bring up the subject of Holland would be suicide for me. 'I will tell him about Holland, I will tell him about Holland,' I said to myself.

The phone rang in the hall. Mum shouted out, 'Astor, is for you.' Dad got up and left the room.

I sank back into the armchair. All the wind had been knocked out of my sails. I felt terrible. I really tried to wait until Dad came off the phone but it seemed he was taking for ever. I got up to go. He came back. 'It's now or never,' I thought, as he sat back in his chair. I took a deep breath. 'Dad,' I drawled. 'Some friends of mine are going to Holland and they are staying overnight and there will be dancing, it really sounds great,' I beamed a big broad smile.

He looked up not saying a word.

'Hmm, and it really only costs forty pounds. Imagine all the cheap wine I could bring back!' I smiled a watery smile.

He took off his glasses. 'Yu nar going, and me nar drink wine.' He put his glasses back on and opened up the paper.

'But Dad, what's wrong with that?' I asked, feeling my confidence coming back.

'I'll tell yu what wrong wid dat. Mi baby daughter going tousans of mile away dance up wid dem dutty wild bwoy, no sah, never will such a ting happen.' He turned back to his paper.

I went back to the window-ledge in my bedroom, I felt like running away but I knew even before the thought was formed that it was impossible. Why were my parents so set against my going? I felt sure they were being wicked.

I could remember when I was only twelve years old my older brother Danny, who was in his late teens, started going out with a string of white girls, going to all-night parties and not coming home for two days sometimes!

My dad had thought it funny, and whenever he saw Danny, usually with a different girl on his arm, he would say, 'I see yu still having fun. When time come fi seriousness, marriage and ting, is black girl yu gwine want,' he joked.

Danny would put his arm round Dad's shoulders and say, 'Dad, when you're in love, that's it, don't matter who it is.' He smiled. Then you'd be lucky to see him again for that week!

Danny chopped and changed his girlfriends more than he changed his socks! I couldn't understand why he mainly had white girls – I mean he was quite good-looking and I'm sure he wouldn't have found it difficult getting a black girl. I wondered if he could love *all* the girls he went out with, or perhaps it wasn't love at all! Whatever it was, he never hung on to them for long. Hmm, love must be blind!

But Dad never seemed to get upset with Danny. Both my parents were polite to the girls that Danny brought home. In fact, they went out of their way to make them feel at home. 'Would you like some tea?' Mum would ask. Dad would ask if they wanted something a little stronger. Everything was rosy until Danny came home with Michelle. We had seen her quite a few times before, but never thought anything of it. Now she was standing with an egg-shaped sparkler on the third finger of her left hand and a beaming smile on her face. Then Danny said that they had just got engaged and we were the first to know. Dad's eyes popped and his tongue nearly dropped out of his head, as if his air supply had been cut off!

'What!' he shouted. 'Yu a go marry her, bwoy, yu a sport!' Dad sucked his teeth.

'Well,' said Mum, folding her arms, rocking back and forth in her chair and pursing her lips, 'all me know is love know no bound.'

'Ooman, hush yu mout.' Dad was beginning to get upset.

An uncomfortable silence followed, nobody wanted to look at anyone else. Mum got up and hugged Michelle, 'Welcome to de family.' she said. Dad walked out of the room banging the door behind him.

They were married soon after that. It was a lovely wedding. I was the only black bridesmaid, but then there were only two of us! Michelle's parents, Jeff and Tina, seemed a bit standoffish at first but by the time we had got through the last toast, Jeff was slapping Dad on the back and Dad was telling him the story about the time he had almost won a treble chance. The best part of it was that they left Danny and Michelle in peace.

After that, I was the only child at home, and I must admit that at that time I loved it, alone with Mum and Dad. Anything that I wanted and asked for in the right way, I usually got. I suppose really that I was a little spoilt, but I made up for it, just being me. When I told my parents that I had decided to stay on at school, they were pleased. I did not feel that I needed to tell them that it was partly because I wasn't sure what to do with my life. I mean, I loved children, I loved animals, I loved dancing, I loved travelling – not that I had done any to boast of – so unless I could get a job as a nanny, who was a part-time vet, who could pirouette up and down the aisle of a 747 jumbo jet, staying on at school was the next best thing. By some miracle I had managed to get eight O levels. Most of my friends only managed about six. We all went on to the same college of further education where I got two A levels.

To say that my parents were pleased was an under-statement. My mum was beside herself. She could not wait to tell her sister, Aunt Bernice who lived in Manchester. As soon as I got my results she was on the phone. 'Bernice,' she shrilled down the receiver. 'Imagine! Marcia just get de results fi her GCE and she pass all of dem.'

I was spreading peanut butter and jam on some toast, and could just picture Mum's face, eyes all sparkling, mouth spread in a permanent grin. Her face would appear to be glowing from beneath the skin, making it look two-tone. I knew she'd look beautiful.

'Yes mi dear, eight O levels. Well, I know fi certain dat her brains come from our side of de family,' she said. 'Eee ee, I agree wid yu Bernice, but den look at Aunt Lou who did av de shop in Princess Street down town, she was like a computer, she add up de money so fast. Remember when Mr Cole try tief 'er, and she cuss im out of de door, and tell im sey ee caan spell C-A-T much less count.' Mum was laughing until tears were running down her face.

Dad was worse. He loved to boast about his children, especially me. He was bad enough when I hadn't done anything, now that I had done pretty well with my O and A levels, he was showing off ' 'bout him Marcia'! I never heard him boast about me personally, but I usually got it second-hand from Sandra, whose dad worked in Dad's electrical shop.

'Marcia, guess what your dad's been saying about you now,' she would giggle. I did not really want to hear, but I knew that whether I did or not I was going to.

'What?' I said, sounding as bored as I could, which never put her off.

'He said that you were going to be a doctor, or something of that standing, perhaps the first black British woman astronaut!' she added, holding her stomach because she was laughing so much.

'Well, you never know, it could happen,' I snapped.

'Oh leave off, Marcia, it's Sandra you're talking to, not an idiot,' she replied.

Secretly, I thought she was jealous, because my dad

was so interested in my life, and loved to talk about it to anyone and everyone who would listen.

Sometimes my parents would treat me like a baby, which really irritated me, but at the time I could not do anything about it. Going out with boys – even though I was nearly eighteen – was very difficult. That was one of the drawbacks of being the youngest child. My parents were always wanting to know my whereabouts; when I was going out, who I was going with and when I was coming back. It was a drag.

When I first became 'friends' with Leon – who I suppose you could call my first serious boyfriend – both my parents insisted that I bring him home. I really dreaded it. I tried to explain to him what my parents were like, but all he could say was, "That's cool darlin,' nodding his head like a puppy dog. Try as I might to prepare him, he would not listen.

Dad liked the look of him at first, even offered him some refreshments. Leon jumped at the suggestion of a glass of brandy. Dad's Five Star! No less! I knew he was a lost cause from then.

'Eem, where was it yu say dat yu living, son?' Dad said.

'Alton Drive,' beamed Leon, the brandy obviously warming his stomach.

'Alton Drive,' mused Dad, mostly to himself. 'In de council flat or de private house dem?' Dad was a terrible snob at times.

'In the private houses,' said Leon.

'I understan dat yu interested in mi daughter?' Dad said gently.

Not having a clue that Dad was sniffing out a stinker, Leon replied, 'Yeah man, she's cool.'

I squirmed in the armchair, just wishing for the floor to open up and swallow Leon whole.

Dad just looked at him. 'What yu studying for? Doctor? Lawyer? Astronaut?' Dad said, hardly moving his lips. He was sitting straight up as though he had a steel rod in his back.

'Astronaut, or maybe a DJ,' smiled Leon, showing himself up for the brainless boy he really was. By now I was feeling that Dad had done me a favour, Leon was right out of my books.

'Good, I like fi see a bwoy hu ave ambition,' Dad smiled with his teeth clenched.

That was the last time I really saw Leon. Dad never stopped saying how he had single-handedly fought off a 'deviler of women' from spoiling his daughter, in the space of five minutes, with the help of a tumbler of brandy.

When I started going to North East London Polytechnic, my parents were ecstatic. I started off quite excited, but it quickly wore off when I discovered that there was no easy way to study. It was really hard for me, simply because I was bored. Most of my friends who had somehow or other got jobs were earning money and were more or less free from their parents' close scrutiny – unlike me. Mum and Dad became more and more interested in everything I did. However, I did not mind when I passed my driving test and they got together to buy me a little Mini – secondhand, but it moved like a rocket. Most of my friends, like Sandra for example, were not so fortunate and still had to rely on London Transport, so whenever we all went out, I became the mini-cab driver.

After the first few months in college, I really settled down and quite liked it. I became very friendly with Afrina, who was from Ghana. She was so brainy. Studying seemed so easy for her. She did not have much family in London, and so we spent a lot of time together.

I took her home to meet my parents. 'Mum and Dad, this is Afrina, my friend from college,' I said.

Dad stood up and shook her hand. 'Pleased fi meet yu,' he said.

Mum nodded her head and smiled. 'Yu here by yurself dear?' she enquired.

'That is correct,' Afrina replied, 'but I don't mind, as I have made a lot of friends who are very kind, especially Marcia,' she said politely.

'Marcia is such a *good* girl,' Mum said, boasting a little. I felt a bit embarrassed the way Mum and Dad were singing my praises. If only they knew some of the things I could get up to they would be so shocked, well perhaps a little surprised. Sometimes Afrina would come round for dinner. My parents loved having her and Afrina usually enjoyed herself. When she went Mum and Dad would go on about how nice she was and what nice manners she had. 'Yu can tell she come from a good family, *well mannasable*,' Dad would often say. They were glad to see that I was not keeping company with undesirables.

I was getting so caught up in activities at college and socialising with my new friends, that I hardly spent any time at home. Mum and Dad did not seem to mind at all. They had become less strict with me and I could virtually come and go as I pleased. Although I am sure if I told them I was going to a blues party – all night long – they would have had a fit! Mind you, I didn't fancy the idea of going to that sort of party then anyway. But after all, I was eighteen and if I wanted could get married without their consent, though the men . . . or rather boys . . . I knew then were not my idea of perfect husbands!

I had been thinking for some time that, as Mum and Dad had relaxed the reins on me, perhaps they would not mind my moving out. Then Afrina told me that the girl she was sharing with had left. I wondered . . . I really felt that I needed to be on my own, looking after myself, controlling my own life. Of course, I would go home as much as possible, especially when I was broke. No, don't get me wrong. I would not dream of using Mum and Dad as a banking facility, but when times were hard. . .

Sitting at the kitchen table, with the smell of the pea soup and succulent dumplings wafting up my nose, was a bad time to tell Mum I was planning to leave home. But I wanted to test the waters so to speak.

'Mum, Afrina is looking for someone else to share her two-bedroom flat with. What do you think?' I enquired.

'Well, me nar know anybody hu would want it, but me find out at work if anybody interested,' she said. 'Afrina such a nice gal.'

Now, I know my mum is not thick, or slow, but I was not sure whether she had cottoned on to what I was trying to say.

'Mum, I, hmm, I thought that perhaps I might take it,' I said, trying to force a lump of dumpling down my throat with maximum effort but little success.

Mum, meanwhile, was having difficulty with some peas that were threatening to cut off her air supply.

'What nonsense yu a talk 'bout ee?' she gasped. 'Marcia, nar worry me wid yur foolishness.' She got up, put a pot cover over her plate, placed it in the oven and walked out of the kitchen.

From that point on things began to change. I could not quite put my finger on what exactly the 'things' were, but I felt different. I spent even less time at home. When I was there, Mum fussed over me and Dad tried to engage me in trivial conversation. This resulted in me avoiding them even more. It sounds awful, but it's hard to feel at ease in a situation that you do not want to be in and you have no control over. The terrible thing was that I knew my behaviour was causing my parents pain. I felt dreadful, but I could not stop doing things that upset them.

Danny asked me over to dinner at his place. I was relieved. At last, I thought, I will have someone to talk to who would be able to understand me and maybe even talk to Mum and Dad.

The evening started off lovely, then we got on to the 'real reason' for my being there.

'Marsh' – that was what Danny called me – 'I spoke to Mum and Dad the other day and they said that you wanted to leave home.'

'Dan, I'm so glad that you understand me,' I said, relieved. Then came the blow.

'Well, I think you should stay put, until you have at least taken your exams and got yourself a job.'

'What? You must be joking. I'm fed up with staying at home, I want to be on my own, what's wrong with that?'

'Listen Marsh, the world's a hard place, and there's really no rush to join the rat race yet,' he said.

I was lost for words. I looked at Michelle, pleading for her to come to my rescue.

'Danny,' said Michelle, 'I can see what Marcia's going through, she needs somewhere to do whatever she pleases and not have to make excuses or justify herself.'

Thank God. Someone who understands me. I felt like one of those stupid girls you read about in those teenage magazines.

'What are you talking about, Michelle? What does Marsh want to do that she needs to hide from my mum and dad?' he asked.

'Well, think back to the time when I sneaked you into my bedroom, and you put the chair up against the door, and my mother wanted to come in, and I pretended to be asleep and wouldn't answer her. Now, that's a good reason for Marcia to want some privacy.'

Danny looked up at Michelle, and his eyes had begun to go red. It was his own built-in danger signal.

'Are you saying that my baby sister sneaks men into her bedroom under my parents' noses?' he hissed at Michelle.

'Before you start accusing me, remember what we used to do,' she hissed back.

I could see that this was going to be the beginning of World War Three.

'Please,' I interrupted, 'let's change the subject. If this is going to cause you to have a bust up, forget it.'

'Marsh, I promised Mum and Dad that I would talk to you,' he said, calming down.

'Well, you can say that you did, and leave it at that,' I said.

It seemed that Mum and Dad were bending over backwards to please me. If I left without making my bed, I would come home to find it made. My room would be tidied for me. Dad kept asking if I had enough money and was the car running okay – I was getting sick of it. Whenever I was at home I felt an urgent need to get out into the fresh air. I felt sure I was beginning to suffer from claustrophobia.

Amazingly, Sandra – and we can trace our friendship way back to nursery – agreed with my parents.

'Marcia, I don't know why you are making all this fuss,' she said, patting her soon-to-be-born baby. 'You have parents who love you, you live in a nice house, you have no responsibilities, you don't have a man to tie you down, in fact you have no problems,' she finished, shrugging her shoulders. I felt I was seeing Sandra for the first time. She'd been working since I went to further education college. She still lived at home, but would soon be getting a little flat with her baby and her permanent boyfriend – even though he was a bit rough. That was where we differed. My maternal instinct had not as yet reared its ugly head. How could she be telling me that I was making a fuss?

'Sandra, I don't think you understand me,' I said gently.

'Understand? Understand! You've lived in a bubble all your life, you would not be able to cope on your own, you'll be lost, and you will still have to be hanging around your mother's skirt-tails, asking for this and that. Just stay where you are until you find your feet,' she shouted.

'Sandra,' I said drily, 'it may have escaped your attention, but we are the same age, and you are not my grandmother.'

'Marcia, we may be the same age, but I am more experienced than you,' she said.

I looked at her stomach and said, 'So I see.'

I left her house vowing never to return.

I felt depressed. It all seemed so crazy. I just wanted to have some space of my own. To do as I pleased – without the watchful eyes of my parents monitoring my every move. Anyone would have thought I wanted to escape to Mars!

One Sunday morning, while the three of us were having breakfast I began to cry for no apparent reason. Mum started crying, too, and Dad kept swallowing even though he did not have anything in his mouth.

'Marcia, when I was yur age I already had two picknee and yur fadda was working very hard, as well as trying fi educate 'imself,' Mum said quietly. 'Our life was really hard, but we tank de Lawd that 'Im gave us de strength to come tru it all. Yu is de last chile at home, and all we want is fi give you a good start in life. Yu is unhappy wid me and yur fadda? Tell us what is trubbling you, please!' she cried.

I was so choked up, I could not speak. Dad turned to me and said, 'Marcia, if yu really want fi leave, we will help you all we can. But we prefer yu stay here wid us. Yu know seh we love yu very much, but is yur choice.'

What could I say to that? I knew that I was not going

anywhere. So I resigned myself to stay at home until I got married.

Then I met Steve.

I was the last one out of the classroom, and was walking down the corridor in a daze when a voice called out, 'Marcia!' I turned but did not recognise anyone, so I kept on walking. 'Hello Marcia.' I heard running footsteps and turned to find myself up against a broad brown chest sporting a gold chain with a half sovereign hanging from it, which moved up and down as its owner tried to catch his breath.

'I've been looking all over the place for you,' he said. 'Tomorrow our sound system is playing in your area and you promised you would come with me if it wasn't too far. Will you come?'

Well, I was shocked. I mean, Steve and I hardly knew each other. I'd met him once or twice in the canteen at the Poly and he was for ever telling me about 'this sound' he helped run and how good it was. At first, I was not particularly interested. Well, all-night parties in a derelict house, and you had to pay to get in; I imagined it pitch black, full of stale sweaty bodies, rubbing up together, and degenerates bombed out of their skulls. And anyway, I thought Steve was just advertising the event in a general kind of way. I had not thought he really wanted me to go to a dance with him. Anyway, everyone knew how strict my father was.

Steve came and picked me up at the top of the road. I did not tell my parents I was going out with him that night, in his dad's car, looking, well, slick. When we got to the house, it was in a respectable street and the house was definitely not derelict. As we walked in, most people said hello to Steve and kept asking (the men, that is), 'Is she your ooman, nice, nice, she look fit.'

It made me feel, hmm, well, pleased. To tell you the

truth, I was right chuffed. I even met a few friends from school and college, and I spied Colleen, who lived a few doors away from me. I went over to her and chatted to her for a while. I really just wanted to tell her not to mention anything to my parents (or hers) that she had seen me. She told me the same thing!

I really had a good time.

In that one night I learnt how to water-pump like an expert, dance with a boy without the fear of being sexually harassed, develop a liking for Babycham and know when the next date was for 'the sound' to play.

I also saw Steve in a different light. He was such a gentleman. He would come over to make sure that I was all right. 'Do you want another drink? Something to eat?'

'No, I'm fine,' I smiled at him.

When I danced with him, what can I say, his movements were so fluid, every muscle under control, he held me lightly in his arms. 'Ooh,' I thought.

I did not realise it was that late, or early depending on which way you looked at it, until I vaguely heard someone say that they were going to catch the last bus! I looked at my watch. Two o'clock. I froze. I walked over to where Steve was and told him I thought that it was time for me to go home. He could see the worry in my eyes.

'My dad will kill me,' I said. I must have looked really scared because Steve stopped sorting the records right away and said something to his friend. He got my jacket from the top of the speaker box and handed it to me, found the car keys and we left.

We half ran, half walked down the path, through the gate and jumped into the car; Steve drove as though he was a Formula One driver. He had to brake a bit sharp a few times, and I thought that as well a seat belt, I should have worn a crash helmet! We had not spoken since we left the house. Steve stopped the car at the top of my road. He drew breath quickly and exhaled. We sat in silence. He took my hand in his and squeezed.

'Parents,' he sighed.

'Where would we be without them?' I smiled. We sat for a time, each holding the other's hand tightly but looking straight ahead, lost in our own thoughts.

'It's only for a time,' I said. 'I want to move out – my parents are so over-protective. You know, I have come to the conclusion that parents, especially mine, cling to their children more as they get older, as though to have the children fly the nest would sever their lifelines.'

'You're right, Marcia. I feel the same way at times, but I do have more freedom than you – but then I'm a boy,' he said. Then he looked deep into my eyes, and I was not sure whether we were supposed to kiss or not. I decided not and told him it was all right to drop me off at the corner, as the car outside the front door might wake Dad. Somehow I managed to sneak in without anyone hearing me. I could hardly believe my good luck.

Sitting on the window-ledge in my bedroom, I thought about the scene with my parents. Was it only seven weeks ago that I'd gone to the party with Steve? If my parents had known, would they have carried on like they are now over this stupid weekend trip? I came back in one piece – I'm positive I'll come back in one piece from Holland! The more I thought about it, the more stupid I felt the whole thing was. Here I was, eighteen years old, being told by my parents that they were not letting me go away for a weekend, because I might get pregnant, hooked on drugs, perhaps even run away! I was hurt by the fact that they did not trust me. They acted as though I was, or had been, a problem child who, if let out of their sight for more than twenty-four hours, would have the police knocking on the door reporting some misdemeanour.

I leaned my head against the window-pane. Tears slowly spilled over and ran down my cheeks. A cloud of depression settled on my head, and inside my emotions were at battle with each other. An hour passed and I did not even realise it, I was so lost in my thoughts. I thought again about moving out. I did not really want to upset Mum and Dad but I knew that I had to take that step; this situation was not going to get any better.

'Right, I'll start at the beginning,' I told myself.

I had no money. I did not even have a Saturday job. The grant I was getting barely covered any of my needs and, once I had left home, I would not want to borrow money from my mum and dad as that would be a sign of defeat. I knew I had to get a part-time job.

I had made my mind up. Now, there was still the problem of the trip. I went downstairs. As I neared the front-room door I could hear Mum and Dad talking, and as I passed it, their voices stopped. They must be discussing me, I thought. I walked over to the phone and dialled Steve's number.

'Hello Steve, how are you? About the trip, I was wondering if it would be possible to give you the deposit a bit later?' He said it would be fine and not to worry. I explained briefly what had happened. He was really sympathetic and told me if he could help in any way, not to hesitate to call him.

I slowly replaced the receiver. I was frantically hanging on to my confidence which was threatening to desert me. Then I thought, why not call Afrina and ask if the room was still vacant? In my mind, it was no longer a question. I had made the decision.

I dialled. 'Hello . . . Afrina . . . It's Marcia . . . it's about the room . . .'

Day Out

Barbara Jacobs

There wasn't much sun, but we pretended there was. We pretended it was still summer. Freewheeling into the bitter wind, we rolled down the hills on our bikes, giggling, making for the grey strip of sea beyond the rooftops.

'Just like old times,' Lisa yelled across at me. Two oranges and a packet of foil-wrapped sandwiches bumped around in the carrier on her bike.

'Yeah,' I agreed, laughing.

It was and it wasn't. Beneath the laughter I was still jealous, tired of having my ear bent by stories of the love of her life she'd met on holiday in Majorca, fed up with her almost daily excuses about how she couldn't come round because she was expecting a phone call from Simon, or sticking her Simon photos in her holiday album. And I was still reeling from the surprise of seeing her standing on my doorstep that morning, out of the blue, and her mum's borrowed bike leaning against our gate.

'Thought it might be a good day to ride to the coast,' she'd grinned.

We rode like maniacs into the wind and the grey autumn sky. Lisa did her old tricks, swinging her goosepimpled legs up to the handlebars as we slid down hills, singing at the top of her voice, trying to make a slipstream of happiness that I had to ride into. I couldn't see that I had any reason to join in. I knew this love of hers was shutting me out.

'Viva España!' she sang.

'Viva Cleethorpes,' I grunted.

'You've got no romance in your soul!'

'Got none in my life, either,' I complained.

'We'll find you one, then. Today. This is the day you discover passion under the summer sun, a love to last the winter long!' she sang.

She raved. I grinned. We swung down through the cobbled streets of the town and parked our bikes in a side street behind the sea front. I carried the cans of coke I'd brought; she struggled, juggling sandwiches and oranges as we raced each other across the road, down the steps, to flop on the shingle of the littered beach.

The wind whipped our hair, and rolled our oranges towards the grey sea. We ran to save them, paddling in the froth at the edge of the waves, squealing with cold. Then we emptied pebbles and seawater from our shoes, and trudged back to our sandwiches.

Lisa peeled her orange carefully and threw the peel over her shoulder. 'Look Val!' she nudged me. 'It's a perfect S. S for Simon. Now you do it. Go on. It's supposed to reveal your secret love.'

'I'm not interested in secret loves,' I grumbled. 'I'm not interested in love at all. It makes you sing out of tune, and wait for phone calls and letters that never come. It makes you stupid.'

But I threw the peel, all the same, and as I did I heard what seemed to be a strangled sob from Lisa, but it could have been just a sniff against the wind. She crawled behind me to examine it.

'Oh,' she said.

'Oh, O!' I laughed at the clumsy circle of orange peel. 'O for zero, zilch. O for nothing at all!'

'O for Orville?' Lisa suggested. 'Or Olaf?'

'Great. Today's the day I fall in love with a duck, or maybe a Norwegian pop star. What do you think?'

'O for 'orrible. Obviously . . .'

I thumped her, and chased her into the sea, then back up the sand. She made a tower of stones and we threw pebbles at it, shivering, as she gave me a beat by beat account of the state of her heart. I didn't know if it was touching or funny. But for the first time since she'd come back from holiday I really listened, drawn into her story of Majorca and this dark-haired boy I'd never met but had decided I hated. I stopped hating him. I started to understand.

'And . . .' she said, finally.

'And?' I prompted.

'I'll tell you after. Let's see if the fair's still open, shall we?' she sniffed.

The fair was half boarded up. We peered through the dark windows of Madame Rosa's booth as the wind rattled the padlock on the door.

'Astrologer to the Famous,' Lisa read, looking at the faded signed photos behind the grimy windows. 'Who's Matt Munroe? Who's Patti Page? Who're the Incredible Flying Zeros? I wanted my fortune read, Val!'

'Rifle range is shut, too,' I grumbled. 'And the Hook-a-duck stall . . .'

A few fairy lights glimmered against the dull sky. A hit from early summer squeaked distantly.

'If the Hook-a-duck stall's closed, you've not got much chance of picking your Orville up, have you?' she said, looking serious for a moment before bursting into giggles.

'It'll have to be a Norwegian pop star, then!' I grinned, hopefully.

'And here he comes!' whispered Lisa, sarcastically, flicking her eyes to indicate that we were being followed. 'With his keyboards player!'

My eyes flicked round, too, just for the second it takes to register that it wasn't worth looking. We were being tailed by two boys in knee-length shorts and loud palm-tree shirts, Vic and Gazzer. We knew they were

Vic and Gazzer because they were desperate that we should know.

'Which one of them two d'you fancy, Gazzer?'

'Tall one's nice, but the little one's got better legs, Vic!'

'Nah, they both got nice legs, Gazzer.'

'D'you reckon we should offer them one of our chips, Vic?'

'Think they're worth it?'

'The legs're worth it!'

'Oi! Girls! How about a chip?' Gazzer asked, running round in front of us, holding out a greasy tray, swimming in a mixture of ketchup and vinegar, and two cold chips. Vic hurtled after him. They stood bouncing in our path like two spotty beach balls. I folded my arms and assessed each one, from dirty plimmies up to the spikes of their greasy hair. I shook my head, slowly.

'Not keen on the legs, Lisa,' I sighed.

'What legs? I don't see any legs. They're on castors.'

'This one's got pointed ears,' I said, poking my finger at Gazzer.

'This one's disguised as a human!' she groaned, waving a hand at Vic.

'He'll never get away with it,' I tutted.

'Not with those green da-glo teeth,' she agreed sadly.

'And the foam-rubber skin,' I said.

'. . . that doesn't quite fit over his knees,' she agreed.

Gazzer and Vic backed off, bewildered, stumbling over their fat feet, spilling the two cold chips, and disappeared into an amusement arcade.

'Nerds!' Lisa sighed.

''Orribles,' I laughed.

'At least Simon's got legs. And he doesn't have a green smile, or pointed ears. Or a Hawaiian shirt,' she sniffed.

'Or chips!'

'That's a point!'

We let our noses guide us to the van, and bought a tray of chips to share, eating them while we walked round deciding what rides we'd have chosen if we hadn't spent our money on chips. Then, arm-in-arm, we walked back down along the wind-swept promenade.

Two kids were aiming empty coke cans at our bikes when we arrived back in the side street where we'd parked them.

'Hey! Lay off!' I yelled.

'What for! They're rubbish bikes,' one kid said, wiping his nose on the sleeve of his parka.

'Got no gears,' the other spat.

'Got no turbo-chargers!'

'This,' Lisa said, grandly, wheeling out her mum's battered bike, and tossing out some empty coke cans from the carrier, 'is a genuine antique bicycle, worth hundreds of pounds.'

'Thousands of pounds,' I said.

'See Darren. I told you we should've nicked 'em,' the little one said.

'Huh!' said Darren.

Lisa and I climbed up and wobbled off, and the coke cans flew after us up the cobbled main street.

All the way back, Lisa was quiet. Me, too. I didn't know what to say about Simon. I felt stupid about the way I'd snapped and snarled and yawned with boredom every time she mentioned him over the last few weeks.

'Maybe we should've given those two the chance to make our wildest dreams come true . . . Gazzer and Vic . . .' I said.

'The twin Aliens?' she laughed.

'Droids. They were definitely Droids,' I said.

'If we'd asked them where they parked their UFO we could've bribed those two kids to nick it!' she laughed.

'Er . . . listen . . . Lisa,' I swallowed, freewheeling.

'About Simon . . .'

'Yeah. I was going to tell you about Simon, wasn't I? I was going to tell you the truth. He never wrote back, Val. He never phoned. I couldn't get any answer when I phoned him. I mean . . . I fell in love with him and all that, but it looks as if it wasn't the same for him . . .' she said, quietly.

'He'll get in touch,' I told her. 'He will. Maybe he lost your address or . . .'

'Holiday romance, that's all,' she whispered.

'Or maybe he's staying with his gran in the middle of nowhere, without a telephone, or maybe he's been ill, or maybe he lost his voice and broke his wrist . . .'

'Or maybe he's been kidnapped!' she smiled sarcastically.

'Yeah, that's it! By Aliens. Maybe Vic and Gazzer. They've probably got him locked in their space capsule, and they're torturing him, mercilessly . . .'

'With cold chips,' Lisa giggled. 'And then they came to look for me, for the ransom. And I never realised. I bet all I had to do was to plant a kiss on Gazzer's spotty cheek and Simon would've gone free. As simple as that!'

'All you had to do was kiss a Droid,' I laughed.

'Don't!' she shuddered, helpless with giggles.

'You could've closed your eyes.'

'He had green teeth, Val!'

'To match his shirt. They're very fashion-conscious in his part of the galaxy,' I told her, giggling, too.

'No more, no more!' she pleaded, pedalling furiously up the hill, and then freewheeling down, singing loudly.

'Hey, next time we bump into two love-sick androids, Lisa, just start singing. That'll shift them!' I called after her, freewheeling too, and joining in with the chorus.

Seeing for Herself

Kanta Talukdar

'Well here I am,' thought Rukmini, 'seeing the promised land at last. At eighteen years of age.' She felt
empty and irritated. She had expected the whole trip to
be a feast of delight. Perhaps it was just being with her
parents all the time and, of course, her four-year-old
sister Rita. She never seemed to have a minute's time to
herself.

Ever since they set foot on India she kept having
arguments with her parents and found it more and more
difficult to like her relations and parents' friends. She
could have sworn that her mother and father had
changed since they landed.

Take that incident in the Bazaar. An old man in a torn
shirt, without any shoes, kept following them around
the shops, begging them to buy some tea towels. After
half an hour of the old man's pleading her father agreed
to buy two but haggled away shamelessly, eventually
getting three towels for the price of one. Then her father
triumphantly announced that he had made a real
bargain. In England the tea towels would have cost at
least four pounds and now he had paid less than twenty
pence for them. It was as if he had put all his pride into
snatching away the old man's profits. Even though the
old man had said he had a family to feed and the
Vasudevas could help him by buying these towels.
Rukmini had mumbled about stealing food from babies
but her father seemed not to hear. Then as he looked at

Rukmini he saw the disapproval on her face and suddenly looked crestfallen. 'It's different here,' he said brashly and hurried the family along the Bazaar with its little stalls bursting with goods for sale.

Images of this Indian holiday filtered through Rukmini's mind. It was almost over. It had been wonderful in so many ways. Smiles had greeted the family everywhere. On the train from Delhi to Calcutta everyone had shared their oranges and puris and samosas with each other. Rukmini had been embarrassed when the lady from four seats away had come along and pinched her cheeks, plonking four more puris on her plate, saying, '*Aare beti*, no objections. Just eat it up, you're far too thin.' Now Rukmini smiled at the memory.

It had been the same on their picnic trip to Diamond Harbour. Rukmini had been speechless looking at the villages nestling peacefully among the wide emerald-green paddyfields. Here and there clumps of banana and mango trees stood guard over the huts. Suddenly mustard blossoms would flash into the countryside, transforming it into carpets of yellow. Just before turning into Diamond Harbour Rukmini caught sight of the Ganges, glinting in the midday sun, bold black specks breaking its glimmering surface.

'Fishermen,' said her father happily. 'We'll have fresh fish for lunch.'

Eating their fresh fish and rice on the river bank a wave of pleasure had overwhelmed Rukmini. Suddenly she had felt the peace of India touch her. Holiday or pilgrimage, Rukmini wondered now. Ever since she could remember, the promise of a trip back home had eased her parents through the problems of settling in a new country. They were always saying, 'In India you would do it like this . . .' despite the fact that home was a dormitory suburb of London and that the family had never been back to India.

*

It was the last leg of the holiday before they flew back to London. Rukmini was glad about this stop at the seaside resort. After all the hustle-bustle of 'seeing India' and meeting relatives it gave her a chance to think things through.

Sitting on the balustrade, looking at the sea, Rukmini turned to see Acchaamma – Rita's ayah – squatting on her haunches, looking rigidly away, her back supported by one of the gleaming white pillars which gave the luxury seaside hotel its Italian villa look. The stiff and awkward angle of Acchaamma's neck made Rukmini think something was wrong. But just at that moment, Rita, sitting on her mother's lap, lunged forward for the jug of water and in seconds all the food on the table was swimming in water.

In a flash, the ever-present waiter sprang into action. The tablecloth was whisked away, Rita dumped on Acchaamma and new plates and lunch organised in minutes. Like a magic show, thought Rukmini wryly. 'Now you see it, now you don't.'

The rest of the day was like every other day of that week. Lunch on the verandah outside the suite, tea on the well-kept lawn of the hotel, under the swishing palms, and dinner in the cosy dining-room accompanied by the low roar of the sea only a few hundred feet away. Rukmini was slightly taken aback at the luxury surrounding her but, seeing her parents accept it so naturally, she decided it was the high point of visiting 'home'.

It felt strange, though, not to do anything for herself. It was something that had been niggling her throughout this trip. There was the time she had watched the thin, fragile body of her Aunt Pushpa's daily help weighed down by the bed sheets she had washed and was taking up to the roof to hang and dry in the sun while the family were drinking tea and chatting. Nobody had thought of helping her. Everyone just carried on talking while the overburdened woman made her way up three flights of stairs to the terrace.

Rukmini wondered if Anil would have just kept sitting . . .

Anil was her cousin. They had been penfriends as children. But the little boy peering impishly out of the photo he had sent then was nothing like the tall, good-looking young man who met them. Rukmini was disappointed when she realised he must have been bullied into picking up the Vasudevas from the station. When her father said, 'So how are things?' Anil's reply staggered them. And it was *her* he was looking at so intently through the driving mirror as he said, 'We don't kill them with bullets but by suffocating their dreams. We deny them their rights and live off their inheritance.'

Later on in the evening there had been an argument. When Rukmini asked Aunt Pushpa about her maid she said, 'It isn't as if we don't want to help, darling. They just don't have any ideas.' She remembered Anil shouting at his mother and saying, 'That's not true. You don't give them a chance. How can they have any ideas about what to do if all their waking hours are filled with finding enough food. When people don't have a present how can they think of the future?'

Aunt Pushpa just raised her hand. 'That's enough, Anil. Believe me, once you are older you will understand more.'

Anil turned and looked hard at Rukmini. 'Why don't you come and see for yourself?' he said.

'Stop it now!' Aunt Pushpa said. 'It's enough that you go off for days on end to this village. Let's talk of other things. Tell me, is it really true that one can telephone from the plane?' she asked Rukmini's father.

The next day Anil was gone but he had slipped a sheet of paper under the door of the Vasudevas' room. Scrawling black ink read, 'In case you want to come and see, my address at the centre is: Gosaba, District Canning, Sunderbans.'

Rukmini was disappointed that she wouldn't see more of Anil. He had seemed to want to talk, to explain things to the family and especially to her. But Aunt Pushpa, seemed quite relieved that he wasn't around all the time. 'Anil wants to turn everything upside down,' she explained to Rukmini. 'Doesn't understand that these things are unimportant. That everyone works hard in their own way. Everyone has their own trials and tribulations.'

But surely some things need to change, thought Rukmini as she looked out into the cloudless blue sky. It just didn't seem fair that some people had everything and others so little. She remembered the barely clothed children with their outstretched arms. That just couldn't be right.

Her eyes wandered back to Acchaamma. Rukmini thought she was beautiful. One of the most graceful women she had ever seen. But it was Acchaamma's face that puzzled her. A kind of sadness seemed to muffle it and, though Acchaamma smiled when she played and sang to Rita, Rukmini sensed that she was often close to tears.

Rukmini was curious about her. One evening as they sat on the verandah drinking tea Rukmini asked her about herself. 'Acchaamma, how many are you in the family?' said Rukmini.

Acchaamma was sitting on the floor. Looking up she said, 'Three,' and looked down again.

'Who are they?' asked Rukmini gently.

'My mother, my son and his father,' said Acchaamma.

'Oh, you have a son! How old is he?' said Rukmini.

'Jayant,' said Acchaamma emptily. 'He's four.'

Acchaamma did not talk freely about herself and Rukmini and her mother had to ask lots of questions before they found out that Acchaamma's husband used to be a fisherman until he fell ill three years ago. Today he just lay around the hut, unable to do anything. Acchaamma could not say what he had exactly, just that the doctor had prescribed good food, better food than he was having. She didn't say much after that, as if it was unnecessary to talk about things that couldn't be changed. She suddenly grabbed Rukmini's legs and started massaging them. Rukmini was startled at first but then she realised that Acchaamma was trying to prove something. That her husband might be disabled and unable to work, but she, Acchaamma was giving the Vasudevas value for their money.

Abruptly Rukmini began to think of England and how comfortable and protected she had been all her life. Taken it all so much for granted, haven't I, she thought. Touching her mother's arms, she said, 'Mother, let's ask Acchaamma to bring her son along tomorrow when she comes to work. Rita and he could keep each other company.' Then, without waiting for her mother to reply, she turned to Acchaamma and said, 'Please bring Jayant tomorrow. I'm sure Rita would love to play with him.' But Acchaamma just stared blankly.

As Acchaamma said *namaste* later on Rukmini brightly reminded her about bringing her child along. But Acchaamma slowly said, 'The hotel people will not like it. It's all right as long as I can go home and feed him at midday.'

The next day, as Acchaamma sat on her haunches, staring pointedly away from the table where Rita was being fed, Rukmini suddenly understood why she always looked away when Rita was being cajoled into eating. She must have thought of her own little son sitting hungrily on the floor, waiting for his two morsels of rice and lentils, and of how she couldn't give him any more.

Rukmini told her parents during lunch what she thought about Acchaamma's grief but was surprised when they didn't reply. Unable to eat, she pushed her plate away. Her mother looked at her soothingly. 'We could give Acchaamma some food to take home with her, Rukmini. Why didn't we think of that?' she said.

Acchaamma seemed happy to take food back home. This lasted for three meals. It was on a still, tropical night that Acchaamma dashed after Rukmini as she started to make the food-pack. The low rumble of the sea, the hundreds of stars piercing the sky and the carefree twanging of crickets in the background infused peace into the night. But Acchaamma was agitated.

'I can't take any of the food home,' she said. 'The bearers caught me on my way out this afternoon and shouted at me. The hotel rules don't allow it.'

Rukmini stiffened. She couldn't believe they had such petty restrictions.

Acchaamma carried on, 'I could tuck the pieces of fish into my blouse and the potatoes in a small bag around my waist. The rest I will have to leave behind.'

Rukmini's mother made her sit down in the bedroom, away from the probing eyes of the room-service staff and eat up the rest. She stroked Rukmini's hair, saying, 'They have to maintain some discipline, darling. How else will they make sure that not all the hotel food is stolen by the staff?'

As Rukmini and her parents sat outside on the lawns late that night, Rukmini was still thinking of the rule. It reflected something that had bothered her throughout this trip. She thought again of Aunt Pushpa's maid, who slept on the stone kitchen floor with only a thin sheet to protect her from the cold, and the layers and layers of blankets that had been piled on the Vasudevas' beds 'in case you feel cold'. It wasn't that Aunt Pushpa was mean or evil, thought Rukmini, remembering her aunt's warm welcome to the Vasudevas. It was as if people who didn't have a similar standard of living weren't worth thinking about, let alone helping. Rukmini closed her eyes in anger and confusion but all she saw was Acchaamma's gentle smile and her sad, pleading eyes.

So poor that they have to *steal food. Steal food. Steal food.* The thought whirred around Rukmini's mind, fanning itself through her being. It was only after she had thought of a way to help Acchaamma that she could go to sleep. At breakfast next morning Rukmini fiddled with the teacup and told her parents of her plan. She began hesitantly.

'You know that money Grandmother left me in her will. Well, I think I want to give it to Acchaamma.'

'Uhhuh,' said her father, slowly nodding his head, drumming his fingers on the table. 'How much were you thinking of?'

She had decided on giving away two thousand rupees. It was a lot of money and certainly a fortune for Acchaamma. But when she told her parents they told her not to tell Acchaamma about it outright.

'Why don't you let your mother have a chat with her. Find out how ill her husband is, can he for instance start a panwallah's shop? Or perhaps he can start a tailoring shop after a little training,' her father said.

'Maybe *she* can do something,' her mother interrupted. 'Her husband might be one of these proverbial drinkers and in one huge drinking spree blow it all up. We must have a long talk with her, Rukmini, and find out definitely what could be done with the money.'

'I think it's a splendid idea, Rukmini. In fact I will put up half the money if you can sort something out. But Acchaamma's husband shouldn't just squander it away.' Her father folded away his napkin deliberately, pressing the folds, driving his thoughts home.

When Acchaamma arrived Rukmini and her mother took her down to the beach to talk to her alone.

'Tell me Acchaamma, what would you really like to do?' said Rukmini's mother, without mentioning the money. Acchaamma just dug her feet deep into the sand and didn't say anything.

'Wouldn't you like to do something else, Acchaamma,' said Rukmini's mother, 'like starting a tailoring shop? Or perhaps your husband can run a panwallah's shop. Does he drink?'

Acchaamma looked up at her and said simply, 'Sometimes he gets very drunk.'

'Well, why don't *you* start a panwallah's shop?' Rukmini's mother said. Rukmini raised her eyebrows. She had never seen a woman in a panwallah's shop.

Acchaamma remained silent. Then she turned toward the sea and the sky. 'There's nothing here, absolutely nothing here,' she said suddenly.

Rukmini was completely taken aback by Acchaamma's lack of plans. When her father asked in the evening what they had decided with Acchaamma, her mother answered before Rukmini could say anything. 'Well, we want to help Acchaamma and her family but she simply doesn't have any plans. We'll just have to give her something more than her salary when we leave,' said her mother as they finished dinner.

The last days at the seaside flew by. Just before leaving, Rukmini's mother called Acchaamma into the bedroom and settled her dues and pressed an extra three hundred rupees into her hands. Rukmini knew it was more than two months' salary for Acchaamma. Acchaamma flung herself at her mother's feet and then at Rukmini's and started crying.

Rukmini stood stock still. She realised that Acchaamma was crying out of happiness. But a slow anger welled up inside her. Why hadn't they given more money to Acchaamma? Why had she let her parents stop her?

Her mother caught hold of Rukmini's arm and said impatiently, 'Come on, hurry up.' She pulled her to the cash desk and paid their bills. Tucking in the two thousand odd rupees change from the ten thousand, her mother led the way to the car. The turbanned doorman clicked the door shut smartly but Acchaamma came forward once again to stroke Rukmini's hair, to say goodbye.

'We'll see you again Acchaamma, take care of yourself,' said her mother brightly, but an overwhelming feeling of disappointment suddenly engulfed Rukmini. She felt this was the only real happening in the whole holiday.

Rukmini brooded as the car sped towards Aunt Pushpa's – the Vasudevas would be spending a night there and catching the plane the next evening. Her failure to help Acchaamma depressed her. Rukmini was very quiet. She refused her mother's constant attempts to make her eat and dug her hands deep into her coat pockets.

Suddenly she became aware that her pockets were not empty. There was something in them. A crumpled sheet of paper. Pulling it out of her pocket she placed it on her knee and smoothed it over with her hands. She was staring at Anil's handwriting, inviting her to the village where he worked. For some time it made her even sadder, to be reminded of Anil. Then an idea came to her.

'Mother,' asked Rukmini, formally; 'international air reservations can be cancelled without losing your money can't they?'

'That's right,' answered her father before her mother could reply.

'Well, I think I'll stay on for a while and come back to Britain in time for next term,' Rukmini said firmly, her mind made up. But secretly she was surprised that her voice didn't tremble.

'How can you stay back in India all alone?' asked her mother immediately. 'Why do you want to do that anyway?'

'I'll keep my things at Aunt Pushpa's, if she agrees,' said Rukmini slowly. 'And go and visit Anil. That way I won't be alone, Mother.'

'And why should we allow you to do that?' said her father. 'You are, after all, only eighteen.'

'That's exactly it,' said Rukmini. 'At eighteen surely I should be able to stay on for a couple of months. It isn't even as if I'll be alone. I'll be with relatives and in INDIA.' Then Rukmini put on her most persuasive voice. 'And Father, you did promise me a present for my birthday. Well, this is what I want. I want to stay on in India and . . . and . . . see for myself.'

Author's note

A *panwallah's shop* is a little street stall selling spices, cigarettes and different kinds of *pan*, a special edible leaf filled with either sweet or savoury fillings.

Aran Sweater
Kerilyn Wood

The blue, stiffly starched cornflower curtains muffled the noises coming from the ward. Jen leant against the edge of the bed and waited. Unsure what to do next. It was only two-thirty in the afternoon.

'Okay, Jennifer?' Jen heard the nurse before she saw her. She was a tall woman. She wore a crisp white apron over purple and white stripes. Jen read her label: Pupil Nurse Mabel Lennox.

'Into bed.'

'Do I have to? Can't I sit in the chair?'

'It's only till the doctor's seen you.'

Obediently Jen undressed, put her pyjamas on and climbed into the bed. The sheets felt clean and cool. Nurse Mabel Lennox pulled the curtains.

In the next bed, an old woman lay with her eyes shut and her mouth wide open. Jen wondered if she was alive or not, and decided she must be or someone would have done something about her mouth. She turned away thinking of open sores, gaping.

'Hello.' The voice belonged to a teenage girl. She was fully dressed in blue jeans and T-shirt. She got off her own bed and hobbled over, picking up a magazine. 'Want something to read?'

Jen smiled and nodded.

'What's your name? I'm Linda Charles,' she said, easing herself on to Jen's bed.

'Jennifer Dawson. Jen.'

'What are you in for?'

Visions of men in white coats. Mad scientist experiments. Operations and exercises. Injections and X-rays. All flashed before Jen's eyes. She knew she couldn't tell the whole story.

'I've got a crooked bone. I think they're going to try and straighten it. That's all.' She waited for some response or reaction, prepared for more questions, but none came. 'What about you?'

'Foot job. Going home soon. Hey! Wouldn't it be great if we could have our beds together, next to one another? I'll ask Nurse Haselgrove when she comes on. She's the staff nurse. How old are you?'

'Thirteen.'

'Oh. You're the youngest here now. It was me, but I'm fifteen. The old ladies are quite nice to you, but they get you to run around after them quite a lot, especially Dolly. That's her, in traction. You do jobs for her, and she just moans that you haven't done it right, or you haven't done it fast enough . . .'

Jen was already afraid of Dolly's bed. Covered by iron bars, pulleys and lengths of rope, with all sorts of metal weights dangling from them, swinging slightly. She now felt afraid of Dolly as well.

'I've not been in the adult ward before. All the other times I've been in, I was in the children's ward. It wasn't like this.' She tailed off, looking over at the woman in the next bed.

Later that night, Jen was awakened from a deep sleep by the sounds of people talking in hushed whispers very close by. The curtains had been closed all around her bed and somewhere a night-light had been switched on. She lay very still, very quietly, listening. Water. Dripping in a bowl. Sounded like a cloth being wrung out. Then the curtain began to move. Gently at first, as if blown by a draught.

She snapped her eyes shut and waited, expecting

someone to come into her cubicle any second. She tried to control her eyelids, stop them flicking, and to breathe deeply and evenly, pretending to be asleep. Nothing happened. She waited a few seconds, then opened her eyes. People were still whispering. She could hear curtains being pulled shut all along the ward. She coughed. The face of a nurse who she hadn't seen before peered through a gap in the curtains.

'Just stay in your bed Jennifer, until the curtains are opened. Nothing to worry about.'

Fear spread thickly through Jen's veins. She knew now that the woman in the next bed had died and they were getting ready to take her body to the mortuary, where dead patients were stored. Jen's mum was a nurse on an old people's ward where a lot of patients died. Jen knew about these things. Even so she felt very scared. Her heart galloped inside her chest. She started to shake. The heat in the ward was stifling. Jen had never been so close to anyone's death before.

'Can I go into Linda's?' She swallowed. Her throat was dry. The curtain on her left side fluttered.

'Nurse, can I go into Linda's please?' She tried to control the rising panic in her voice. The nurse put her head round the curtain.

'Put your dressing-gown and slippers on.' She led the way to Linda's cubicle, parted the curtain and guided her in. 'Now you girls stay here until the curtains are opened.'

'I'd sooner be in yours,' said Linda, as Jen sat on the bed beside her, 'you can tell what's happening.' Jen looked at Linda and shuddered.

'She's dead,' said Linda. 'They thought she might go last night. They were working on her all night long.'

'I don't think I want to sleep in a bed next to somebody who's died,' whispered Jen.

'She's dead, she can't hurt you. People have died in your bed.'

123

Jen looked at Linda.

'Well you don't think they buy a new bed for everyone, do you? You are silly. They just wash the bed, make it up for the next one and carry on as if nothing happened. Didn't you know that? I thought you knew that. You've been in hospital before.' Linda was grinning.

Jen fought back tears as she remembered a small boy on the children's ward. He had died quietly. They had taken him away quietly. One day he was there, laughing and gurgling from his strange cot, designed especially to support his brittle bones. The next day he wasn't.

That was the day she had learned that not all children leave hospital alive and cured. She spent a long time afterwards asking questions. About death. About heaven. She discovered not everyone believed in it as much as she did. Some people didn't believe at all. She was completely shaken. First she had lost Santa. Exposed as a fraud. Somebody's dad in fancy dress. Now she had lost God. Another fraud. She had been led to believe in God by people who didn't believe themselves. Adults were not to be trusted. They lied.

The next morning the nurses moved Linda's bed to where the old woman's had been, with Staff Nurse Haselgrove's firm command that they were not to 'mess about', whatever that might mean.

Linda often had bad moods. Jen found it hard to keep on the right side of her. She was convinced Linda thought her both too stupid and too young because she was not interested in boys. Jen had kept quiet about not liking them much at all. Linda was the only other patient in the ward anything like her age. So Jen went along with her.

'Would you write to me?'

'Don't be daft. You can't write with your arm in a

sling. I *might* come and visit you. I might . . . or I might not. I'll bring my boyfriend. Or I might not if he doesn't want to come. Have to wait and see.'

'Be nice if you did. I don't expect I'll get many visitors. My mum lives in Stepney. It's a long journey. She's got five other kids to get on buses and trains with. I don't think she'll come. Except at the weekend. And my dad works really long hours. He doesn't get home from work until visiting time's over.'

Early the next week, Jen and Linda sat playing cards on Jen's bed until Linda's parents came to collect her. Jen saw them first. A smartly dressed woman wearing a navy blue suit and carrying a small white vanity case, followed by a silver-haired man wearing glasses.

'They're here. Your mum and dad.'

Linda turned. Jen watched her push all the cards into a pile, completely forgetting the game they were half-way through, which Jen was winning. Linda scooped them up and put them back in their box, picked up the box and went over to her bed.

'Hello Mum. Daddy.'

'Hello Linda, are you all ready? Oh hello Jen. How are you today?'

Jen was about to answer when she realised they weren't either looking at her or waiting for her to reply. Mrs Charles was bending down clearing out all the things from Linda's locker, while Mr Charles was leafing through a magazine he'd just picked up.

'Linda, you don't need all this old stuff . . . You won't use it. We'll only be carrying it home to throw it away . . .'

'Oh Mum!'

Linda was interrupted by Mrs Charles. 'Why don't you give it all to your little friend there? We'll buy you some new ones on the way home.'

Linda took the bundle of odds and ends, clothes and

books her mum thrust into her hands and hopped over to Jen's bed.

'You might as well have all this. Mum says she'll buy me all new things on the way home. Oh, no, you can't have those though.' Linda took back the pack of cards they'd been playing with: 'I'm taking these home.'

'I'll miss you,' said Jen.

'Yeah, well, you won't be in here for ever.'

'Hurry up Linda. Say goodbye to your friend. The taxi's waiting. Goodbye Jen. I hope you'll be going home soon.'

Linda punched Jen on her good arm. 'See ya.' Then she went over to her mum and dad. Jen, waiting to wave, watched Linda limp away down the corridor and out through the door. She didn't turn round.

Jen felt an enormous sigh mount up in her chest. She wanted to pull the curtains round her bed, fall on it and have a good cry but she knew she wasn't allowed to close them.

'Jenny.' Jen went over towards Dolly's bed. She wasn't afraid of her or the traction any more.

'Your friend gone?'

Jen nodded, biting back the tears. She didn't want to cry in front of Dolly.

'Do me a favour, love. Fill up my water jug. I'd ask the nurses but they're ever so busy, poor loves. Don't mind, do you dear?'

'Of course not.' Jen knew where to fill the jug. She'd done it many times with Linda. She walked down the ward to the little bathroom off the side. The door was shut. Locked. Jen stood still wondering what to do next. She walked back to Dolly's bed with the empty jug.

'I'll do it for you later. There's someone in there.'

'There's another tap,' said Dolly, 'at the far end. Round the corner, I think.'

Jen didn't want to wander to unfamiliar parts of the

hospital, afraid she might accidentally stumble across the mortuary. Death was always happening somewhere. She took a deep breath and set off up the long narrow ward. It soon seemed like miles away from her own bed. She felt like a nervous intruder going into somebody else's home. She could hear women's voices, calling.

As she turned the corner, she expected to find another bathroom. Instead, she discovered side wards: one on either side of the corridor, with the doors open, facing each other.

From where she stood, Jen could see a woman in bed in each room. The rooms were tiny. The beds were placed in such a way that the patients could not see each other.

Anxiously, Jen put her head round one of the doors: 'Hello.' A woman wearing a crocheted bed-jacket sat up in bed. She wore thick powder, bright blue eye-shadow and red lipstick. Her face was a bit yellow and didn't look quite real to Jen. Her eyes were very bright. Jen thought she must be very old.

'Excuse me, I'm looking for the drinking tap.'

'Well come in, dear. Let's have a look at you then.' She shouted to the other room, 'We don't get many visitors up this end, do we Flo?' Turning to Jen, she asked, 'When's your birthday?'

'May the eighteenth. Where's the water tap please?'

'Ah!' said the woman, nodding slowly: 'Taurus. Taurus the Bull. Slow to anger. Ploddingly faithful. Loyal to the end. Reliable, though.'

'Am I?' Jen smiled, not knowing what else to say. 'Oh.'

'What's your name?'

'Jennifer. Jen.'

'Well, Jen, I'm Mrs Rice. Now why don't you go and fill up your bucket my dear Liza? The tap's in Flo's room. She won't mind if you use her water supply, as long as you don't use it all.' Mrs Rice winked one of her blue eyelids. 'Take your bucket back to whoever it belongs to, and come back and talk to us. We are cast out and forgotten up here.'

Jen crossed from one room to the other. 'Excuse me,' she said to Flo whose fingers clicked away automatically over a pile of thick white wool.

'You go right ahead dear, don't mind me.'

Jen filled up the jug.

'Come back now, mind.'

'Okay.'

Jen went back to the ward carrying the jug, careful not to spill a drop on the floor, and placed it on Dolly's locker.

'Took you long enough,' Dolly grumbled. Jen ignored her and went back to Mrs Rice and Flo. As she approached, she heard another voice. She coughed and walked into Mrs Rice's room.

'Ah! Here she is! Ann, I'd like you to meet our visitor from the outside world. Ann of Aries, meet Jen, Taurus.'

Ann Peyton wore the white uniform and red belt of the physiotherapy department. She smiled at Jen: 'I was coming to visit you later, Jen. Work out some exercises for you, stop your arm getting stiff.'

'Oh-oh! Once she gets her hands on you, you've had it. She'll wind your arms round and round in their sockets till they fall out. You mark my words,' warned Mrs Rice.

Jen sat on a chair by the door and listened to them teasing each other and laughing.

'Did you see what's for supper?' Mrs Rice asked Jen. 'Can smell it a mile away. Or is it Rose washing down the sluice again?'

'Bread and gruel for you for being so ungrateful. What do my stars say for today?' asked Ann.

Mrs Rice picked up her newspaper and read out all the

day's forecasts. 'I'm Scorpio, myself. All sex and death,' she told Jen with a twinkle in her eye. 'Mostly death at my time of life, dear, not much sex. Not much *sex*, is there, Flo?' She called across the corridor.

'Not in front of the youngster, Lily!' Flo's voice came back.

Jen laughed. 'I'm on the adult ward now. I've seen a bit of death.'

'Well you won't see any sex, that's for sure.' Mrs Rice's heavily made up face crinkled. Jen noticed the cracks in the powder.

'I have to go to supper now, but I'll be back.'

'Be sure you do dear. Send the paper boy on up if you see him. Don't think much of the stars in this one. Let's find out what the others have to say.'

Jen spent day after day in the side wards. Linda never came to visit. Jen didn't miss her.

Flo was bedridden. Her legs were just about done in by arthritis, but her hands and fingers were still agile enough to click and pull the stitches into shape. She was knitting an Aran sweater for her nephew who lived close by but never came to visit her. Mrs Rice said she should sew the cuff holes up and elasticate the neck, so when he put it on he would be trapped inside and slowly strangled by it. Flo just arched her eyebrows and said nothing.

Jen watched the knitting grow day by day, fascinated by the cabling that weaved in and out, snaking its way first in front then behind and then in front again. She enjoyed the different textures of the raspberry-like bobbles and the lines criss-crossing over. Often Flo would pass it to her and tell her to do a row while she polished her glasses, blew her nose, or took a sip from the orange juice that Jen made up for her. She was patient with Jen's mistakes.

Late one night Jen's dad came to see her. They sat, not

saying much, playing cards. Jen won a couple of pounds at Newmarket, then they stopped. Money was very scarce. At home, they played for matchsticks. Fares to the hospital were very expensive. He knew Jen would not take any money from him, and she knew he let her win. That was the agreement. It was unstated, unwritten, but binding. . .

'What do you want me to bring you?' he asked.

'Some old wool from the wool bag, and some of Mum's knitting needles. Big ones! I'm going to knit a scarf.'

'Can you knit with your arm in a sling?'

'If I can balance my arm right, I can do anything.'

His visits were rare, not just because of the travelling difficulties and the cost, or that he was needed at home, or even that they had nothing much to say to each other. She had inherited more than just grey eyes from her dad. He had given Jen her crooked bones, and they both knew it.

Jen's scarf was nowhere near finished by the time she was ready to leave hospital, but Flo had shown her how to cast off the stitches, and they'd cut and joined the lengths together. Just enough to go round Flo's hot water bottle. Jen embroidered Flo's name with a strand of her thick white wool.

When she went home, Jen started to knit an Aran sweater for herself. She often thought about Flo and Mrs Rice and once, when she went back to Outpatients for a check up, she dropped in to visit them.

'How's your knitting going?' Flo asked.

'Oh slowly. I'm not very fast, but it is growing. I'm sorry I can't come and see you again. The journey's too far and my mum can't really afford the fares.'

Flo smiled.

'Bah!' said Mrs Rice. 'You don't want to spend your time with us old crocks. You're young. You should make more friends of your own age.'

Much later, Jen finished her sweater. She was very proud of it. It was faultless. Not a stitch out of place. She had designed it with one arm three inches shorter than the other. The doctors had finally taken the staples out of the bones in her right arm, but it had stopped growing. She modelled the sweater in the craft competition being run by the school and won the second prize.

Well, Well, Well
Kate Hall

'Well you obviously can't keep it.'

'What do you mean, CAN'T keep it? Who says I can't?'

'It's obvious – you'll have to have an abortion.'

'I don't want an abortion, I want to . . .'

'You can't, just think about it for a minute.'

'I have thought about it, I've thought about it a lot.'

'But you've just started college.'

'I know I've just started college but there's a crèche there.'

'Oh, I see, you're going to go in pregnant and have the baby in between lectures.'

'It's due in the holidays and anyway I can get time off, other people have done it before, you know.'

'That's doesn't mean you have to, though, does it. And what about money?'

'I'll manage.'

'What, on a grant, with a baby and no father.'

'Yes on a grant, with a baby and no father – that's what's really worrying you, isn't it? Bloody hell, in this day and age!'

'Well it would help if you would say who the father is, or don't you know?'

'Of course I know, but I don't want him to.'

'Why not for Christ's sake, he ought to pay for it – you could get maintenance you know or he could pay for an abortion.'

'I don't want him to pay for anything and I am NOT

having an abortion.'

'He's not married is he?'

'No, he's not married.'

'Then I don't see . . .'

'I just don't want anyone interfering, that's all.'

'Well you needn't worry on my account – I'm not having anything to do with it and don't expect me to baby-sit either.'

'No one asked you to.'

'Not yet, but you just wait. Honestly, I thought YOU were old enough to know better. It's embarrassing.'

'You'll be saying "What will the neighbours say?" next.'

'I don't give a damn about the neighbours but they will think things if there's no father.'

'There is a father!'

'Oh yes, an anonymous one.'

'I KNOW who he is.'

'Well at least tell me.'

'No. Look, I made a decision, I got pregnant on purpose. I want to have this baby, okay?'

'BUT MUM – at your age!'

The Night Run
Sigrid Nielsen

'I kept you under stone, I kept you under steel. I kept you underneath the world for a thousand years.'

The pale golden wolf willed herself not to listen. She leapt along the black battlements, feet burning on the sorcering-ice, with a balance humans never feel.

'You will not escape. The Binding Words have put you under my curse for ever.'

The sorceress' voice in her mind was horribly strong. Desperate, she searched for the true stars over Crosstan, over her home.

Just then the sorceress appeared, dressed in grey, faint light shining from her fine, cruel features. Too late, Cathoren abandoned the wolf-shape for her real self, just as the sorceress' lips opened on the Chant of Eternal Domination.

*Cathoren of Crosstan, robed in bla*ᵏ*e and silver, tossed her hair in the bitter wind and laughed defiance . . .*

'Bugger.'
'Ratbag.'
'Shitebrain.'
Catriona tumbled back to earth. Blushing.

The two boys were waiting for her, as they had done every afternoon for a fortnight now. Usually it was just horrible language and threats: today they had a dog who looked like an old sheepskin carpet, and a box of matches.

Hello? Universe Taxis? I'm in Lomax Road. Going to

135

Crosstan. Beyond the fifth dimension of improbability. And hurry.

Would anyone really burn up a dog on an ordinary schoolday, even in Lomax Road? Catriona had no talent for guessing what people would or wouldn't do. She set her schoolbooks down on the kerb, waded into the street and hoisted the dog up.

Trouble started in less than a quarter of a second. The boys hooted. A car came round the corner too fast and barely missed her.

'Piss off,' said somebody loudly.

Catriona turned to find herself facing a girl with dark spiky hair. 'I was just trying to –'

'Trying to get yourself smelling like a rubbish tip.' The girl gave her a look as if Catriona were some extinct animal she'd discovered in the street. 'Go on, put him down before he really gives you something to remember him by.'

The dog, unaware of being rescued, was struggling feebly in Catriona's grasp. He did have a bit of a stink. Catriona put him down on the pavement and saw that the boys had done a bunk. Could the girl have been telling *them* to piss off? Catriona had no interest in finding out. This kind of girl was trouble. She searched for her books and then saw that the girl had picked them up. And worse yet, was holding up the paperback on the top of the pile.

Oh, no, no, no, no, no, please not that.

'Is that science fiction?'

'I'm – I'm awfully late, if you don't mind.' Catriona stretched out her hand to take the book. The girl held on to it.

'You're covered in dog hair, you know.'

'I am?'

'Come inside and clean yourself up. You won't be wanting to go home like that.' It wasn't quite an invitation. More of an order.

'Thanks awfully for your help,' began Catriona, but the girl had already turned around and started across the street, still holding all her books. In her black lace-up boots, black trousers and black jacket, she walked like a cat burglar.

Cathoren of Crosstan, you don't know the half of it. You are under a curse. You're being invented by Catriona Gough. And her luck is as good as a return ticket on the Titanic.

Catriona's mother had warned her never to loiter in Lomax Road, but the girl's house was very ordinary. It had a garden full of marigolds and the kitchen smelt of fresh paint. A note on the kitchen table read, 'Annie I need 2lb onions, 1lb carrots, 2 tins tomatoes & bread, Love Mum.' Outside the tiny kitchen window, two boys were playing in the back garden. Catriona could see the hill and the outlines of the roofs in her own street in the distance.

The girl picked up the note and a packet of biscuits, and ate one. 'Well,' she said, '*is* it science fiction?'

'Possibly.' Catriona was getting annoyed. The girl was trying to get a rise out of her. She knew what was coming next: *I hate those monster stories. The people have stupid names. And the places are even more daft. Nowhere sensible, like Scotland. Me? I just read* Jackie *like everybody else. Ha ha ha ha ha.*

'I've seen you with sci-fi at school,' said the girl.

All at once Catriona realised where she had seen the girl before. It was at some sort of prize-giving last month. Catriona couldn't remember it, since she had been scribbling a Crosstan story the whole time. Catriona never got any prizes, only lines.

'It's *not* science fiction,' she said stubbornly.

'Maybe it's just the way you wear your uniform,' said the girl, 'like something from another planet.'

Catriona felt her whole face go bright red with anger. 'Do you always eat biscuits without passing them round?' she shot back.

'I'm waiting for you to wash your hands,' said the girl coolly.

Catriona turned away quickly and looked for the soap. When she turned around again the girl was holding the science-fiction paperback. It had a woman with cats' eyes and snakes for hair on the cover.

Catriona pasted a stupid, angry smile on to her face. '*Shambleau*, by C.L. Moore,' she said in a sing-song voice. 'Now may I go, please, miss?'

'You mean Catherine Moore,' said the girl.

Catriona stopped dead. She didn't know what to say. She felt as if she'd just come out in another part of the space-time continuum. A girl like this couldn't possibly have heard of C.L. Moore. *Nobody* had heard of C.L. Moore. This battered short-story paperback was Catriona's only proof that C.L. Moore had ever existed. She had scoured through the secondhand bookshop every Saturday morning for two years without finding any other trace. For a girl like this, who rushed home from school to put on her boots and trousers and make her hair stand up with gel, to know about C.L. Moore meant that the world was an even stranger place than Catriona wished it were.

'Do you *like* science fiction?'

'It's all right,' said the girl. 'Have a biscuit.'

Very slowly, Catriona reached out and took one. She stood there holding it.

'Do you – do you know C.L. Moore? Do you read Jirel of Joiry?'

'What's that? Some kind of comic?'

'No, it's the heroine she writes about, C.L. Moore I mean. She's a warrior who has magic adventures. Jirel, I mean. Didn't you read the book?'

'No, I just tried to nick it once. The old cow in the

shop got really bloody. I had to pretend I'd forgotten.'
She put on a soft refined voice and said, 'Dreadfully
sorry. Awfully embarrassing.'

I'll bet that's just a story, thought Catriona. She could
never tell when people at school were telling stories, so
she laughed noncommittally.

'If you haven't read the book, how do you know
about C.L. Moore?'

'If you hadn't been trying so hard to rush off, I'd have
shown you ten minutes ago.'

The girl led her down the hall past the living-room to
the far door. 'The box room. It's all mine.'

It was a long, narrow, shadowy room, but Catriona
only noticed that a moment later. All she saw was the
bookcase. It towered nearly to the ceiling, and it was
filled with science fiction. There were secondhand
paperbacks and there were cardboard-covered hardbacks from the really old days. There were Star Trek
and Blake's Seven and The Prisoner novels. There were
some Catriona had always wondered about, like *Red
Shift* and *The Dark is Rising*.

'All right, isn't it?' said the girl modestly. 'I put the
shelves up. With some help from Dad. These were my
gran's.' She touched the old hardbacks. 'She's the one
who told me about C.L. Moore. She said her stories
were weird but, you know, real. Like you're really
there.'

Catriona took a bite out of her biscuit. It had
chocolate bits. She'd be out in spots tomorrow. She ate
the rest.

The door slammed in the kitchen.

'Annie!' came a woman's voice. 'Where's the vegetables?'

'Listen,' said the girl quickly, 'could I borrow –
Shambleau? I could have it back by Friday.'

'Well –'

'Tomorrow. If you're going to be stroppy about it.'

139

'Friday's all right.'

'Chum you up the road,' said the girl. 'I'm Anne Ogilvie. You're Catriona, aren't you?'

Why do I feel as if I know her? thought Catriona as she walked home up the hill. *Daft. At least I didn't tell her about Crosstan. She isn't half stuck on herself. Brain box or no brain box.* Maybe she hadn't seen Anne at the prize-giving. More likely, she'd seen her in Crosstan. She was exactly the type.

Maybe she's one of the Five Queens. Maybe she's the Keeper of Crystalcant Mountain. (Not that she'd known Crystalcant Mountain had a keeper until this moment.) She pictured Anne in half-armour, hand-stitched boots, her hair spiky with gel and a dagger in her hand.

The hill was getting steeper. Catriona's house stood at the top, where the road divided. It had a commanding view down the hill. Looking up at the kitchen window, Catriona saw the curtain move.

'It's quite good you're not any later, Catriona,' her mother said as she came in.

'I'm sorry, I didn't stop long . . .'

'The boys across the street have been home for an hour and five minutes.'

Mrs Gough was dressed in her suit and heels. Stomach sinking, Catriona realised this was the afternoon for the Ladies' Altar Guild meeting. Her mother's coat was neatly laid on a chair by the door, and her handbag, with its heavy gold clip, rested on the satin lining; she was just on the point of leaving.

'I'm going to be late now, but I waited so that you wouldn't be locked out.' She put on her coat and gloves and extracted her car keys from the bag. 'Catriona, what's that smell on your jacket? Where *did* you go all afternoon?'

'It wasn't actually all afternoon.'

'If you can't answer a perfectly civil and reasonable

question, Catriona . . .'

'I met a girl – from school. She won a prize last term. She showed me her book collection.'

'She must have quite an extraordinary book collection.' Mrs Gough wrinkled her nose. 'Where does she live?'

'Lomax Road.'

'How nice,' said Mrs Gough, shutting her bag with a steely click.

Catriona pictured Anne and her mother at the dinner table. '*What does your father do, dear? What sort of career do you have in mind?*'

'*I'm going into pryotherapy, Mrs Gough. Help for people who ask too many questions.*'

Catriona sighed. 'Cheerio, Mum. Have a good meeting. Sorry I was late.'

'Don't mention it,' said Mrs Gough, shutting the door hard.

Catriona took her off her jacket and sniffed it. *She* couldn't smell anything. 'Is life possible without luck as we know it?' she said aloud. 'Tonight we interview Catriona Gough, who has survived, totally without luck of any kind, for fifteen years.'

On Friday morning at school a small lithe girl with well-brushed, neatly tied hair and a deadpan face walked up to Catriona and handed her a package.

'That's it back. It was great. See you sometime.'

The bell rang. Catriona didn't get a chance to open the package until lunchtime. It was *Shambleau*. As she opened the cover, two pieces of paper fell out.

One was the Crosstan scene she'd been writing the day she had met Anne. The other was a note.

Dear Catriona [it said],
   Ta very much for the book. Jirel is great. But she should say, 'Stand aside, varlet, or off comes your

head,' more often.

I found this in the book. It must be yours, so I left it.

Anne

P.S. I've never known anyone who wrote stories. Is it hard? If you don't show them to anyone, don't bother but I read yours and I think it's got much more excitement and danger than Jirel. That is a hint.

I will be home early today so phone me *before* 4.00 – 588–0551.

Dear Anne [wrote Catriona],

I guess it's hard to write good stories. It's not hard to write my stories because they don't have a beginning or an end. I'm trying to write an episode of Crosstan for you, but don't blame me if you die of word poisoning. Anyway, this is the background.

Crosstan

Crosstan was ruled by the Ancient Wise who knew the Living Words. In the right combination the Living Words can grow into Time and Space and change them. Don't tell me this is nicked from the Earthsea Trilogy. It's different. The right combinations of Words are called Chants and to use them you have to be a sort of poet. Then Eravang, the evil sorceress, came along. She uses a different kind of magic that makes everything unreal. The Wise left, wanting to avoid scenes I suppose, but Eravang captured one of them, Cathoren, who was young and not fully trained, and put her under a curse. Meanwhile Eravang became the most powerful person in the land and the Darkentime began.

The Darkentime is where it's always 9 p.m. on Sunday night, and you never have your homework done. Just like now. I'd better stop.

Catriona

P.S. I phoned you on Friday afternoon at quarter to four but your Dad said you were busy.

Dear Cathoren [said the note Anne handed Catriona a week later],

Thanks for the bit of your story Catriona wrote out for me yesterday. To be honest, I hope you're never rescued. Tough on you, but then the story can go on for hundreds of episodes. Every day. Well, it beats telly, doesn't it?

Tell Catriona I will write her a longer letter as soon as I finish geometry, French, and lives of the great ratbags.

Anne

P.S. I will try to phone as well but not for too long, Dad rabbits on about the bill.

Well Met In Light And Silence [wrote Anne],

Tonight I took out my file of your letters and the story, I can't believe I've only known about Crosstan for six months, seems like years (about three thousand).

It's a bit much your mum reading my letters, I hope she can read Crosstaren script, ha, ha, but anyway if you want to keep them at my place feel free. I appreciate anyone who wants to be my fan, tell her she can have my autograph.

My dad says I can't go to the secondhand place with you next Sat. He wants help turning the dirt over in the garden (how exciting!! I can't wait). He can get stuffed but I might be late, or if you like you can turn up and hear language that will make the crocuses grow backwards.

What you said about my having a character . . .
What are you on about? I don't get it. She'd have to
be an expert fighter, brilliant, skilled in all the magics,
dead goodlooking, to be anything like me. No,
really, I don't know why I have to have a character.
You don't have one, they're all coming from somewhere else, sometimes I feel you don't see much
difference between here and Crosstan but as far as I'm
concerned they're completely separate. Anyway,
write me a scene about her if you want to but she's
just another character, she's NOT ME.

Go By The True Stars,

Anne

Catriona waited until the dishwasher was making such a
row that no one could possibly hear her. Then she
dialled Anne's number.

'Hi ya. All quiet on the front?'

'They're all watching telly. What about this *woman*?'

So she does want to know, thought Catriona.

'*THE KEEPER OF CRYSTALCANT*,' she read.
She could feel her heart beating. '*The dark-purple sunset
sky was full of drifting clouds, and Cathoren, watching from
her terrace, knew the colours portended deeply troubled days.*'

The scene seemed to go on and on. Catriona realised
that she really did say things longwindedly. Having to
read in a low voice and get it over with before the
dishwasher finished soaping was the way to make sure
you didn't say things more than once.

Anne didn't help either. She kept making silly
remarks or shouting so loud with laughter that her
father would probably hear.

'You haven't said anything about her yet!'

'Hang on, I'm just getting to it. "*You are in danger, and
you must seek the Keeper of Crystalcant out at once. None has*

*seen her in a hundred years, but you will know her when you
find her. Do not delay, for something terrible threatens you –'''*

The phone made a funny wrenching sound. Then
Anne's voice, suddenly fainter, yelled, 'Leave off!
What're you –'

'Anne?'

'You can put that phone down right bloody now,'
said Anne's father's voice.

'Piss *off*,' snarled Anne.

The phone went dead.

Catriona sat holding the phone until she realised it
wasn't going to come back to life. Her own mother
would never have made such a scene. She would have
walked through the kitchen with a ticking timer and a
sign reading, 'You have two more minutes.'

'My dad's not violent,' Anne had explained before.
'He just hits us with his belt and carries on. Dougie and
Grant, they think it's a game, they call it "The Chase".
He hasn't touched me since I was twelve. That's when I
knocked him over.'

Catriona looked out the window and down the hill,
just as though she had Cathoren's chant-sight and could
see into Anne's house. But it was dark and she wasn't
even sure which Anne's window was. *Of course she's all
right*, said the kind, sensible voice in her head, kindly
and sensibly. *And you have four pages of chemistry
homework.*

Back in her room, she picked up the book. It was as
heavy as a rock, and suddenly Catriona felt like
throwing it through the window.

'Well, maybe she *is* all right,' she said aloud, 'but at
least she ought to be able to read the story.' Suppose
Anne decided she didn't want a character of her own
before she saw the end of the scene? And besides, it was
so *bloody* unfair, she'd worked so hard to create
somebody different from the rest of Crosstan, someone

who really was like Anne.

A thought struck her. She walked to the window and opened it. A long time ago she had rested the old ladder up against the wall, just because she liked the idea. No one had noticed and the ladder was still there. She reached down and touched it. Then she grabbed up her jacket. She put it on and stood there with her hand over her mouth. Was she really going to do this?

She thought of Anne. Anne wouldn't hesitate. If you were going to make someone up, you had to feel the way they felt. She climbed over the sill.

You can always go back now, said the kind and sensible voice.

The ladder teetered as she climbed down. She shivered with the breeze at the bottom; or maybe it was fear. It was a really stupid thing to do. It was so stupid that no one but Catriona would go through with it. If she were caught out of the house without permission, her mother might keep her in for weeks, or even force her to go to the hairdressers.'

She looked up at her lighted window, watched her tastefully patterned curtains blow out, then in. She shook her head. Looking up at the kitchen window, she saw her mother. Then she realised it was the reflection of a tree branch in the glass.

Her fingers were shaking so hard that she fumbled the gate latch. It came down with a clank that echoed up the street. She froze. A door opened. She waited for the clack of her mother's high heels on the drive. 'Catriona, what are you doing out here?' But the door slammed. It was someone up the street, letting the cat out. She tried the latch again; it opened, and she was free.

The street was deserted. There was no sound but the cars on the main road far away. It looked like a set for the sort of film where everyone else in the world has been wiped out. She ran down the hill.

She was almost too dizzy to give the secret knock on Anne's window.

She had run without stopping. She kept thinking, *Maybe this is the moment they're finding me gone.*

Then there was a loud scraping sound. Anne was opening the window. She'd been getting on with study as usual.

'Hi ya. A bit late, aren't you? Come in for some tea.'

Catriona was gasping for air. 'No . . . no thanks . . . I . . . I just –'

Anne's face lit up. 'Did you bring the story?'

Catriona looked in her jacket pocket. Then, with a shock, she realised she hadn't brought the story.

'No,' she said. 'No. I . . . I came to see . . . if you were all right.'

Anne looked puzzled. 'Why?'

Catriona was managing longer gasps now. 'You are all right?'

'Oh, I suppose. You mean Dad? Just the usual carry-on. Why're you panting like that?'

'I ran all the way. I've sneaked out, actually.'

'Oh,' said Anne. She seemed to be a bit at a loss for words. 'Well, you'd better get on then. I'll see you tomorrow.'

'Right, and you might not.'

'Don't be daft! How do you know they know you're gone?'

'Just my luck, I guess,' said Catriona.

They were both silent for a moment.

'Off you get, then, it's cold,' said Anne and banged down the window. On the other side of the glass she gestured furiously. Catriona managed a wave and a wobbly leap over the marigolds.

It was all over now.

Catriona ran up the road. It banked by the church, then straightened for the last climb. On the lawns under the street-lamps, the dew shone like beds of diamonds.

She had thought second wind was a joke before, but it wasn't. She had finally learnt to run. It was a bit like flying. She thought of a story she had read for class, one of the few things she had ever liked that wasn't science fiction. It was about a pilot drifting above the moonlit clouds with a few minutes' worth of petrol left and a hurricane below. He knew exactly what was going to happen. He didn't care. It was freedom that mattered, not what was going to happen next. Catriona tried dreamily to remember the name of the story, but it wouldn't come back. Night Run. The Night Run. Something like that.

She got to the top of the slope where the road dipped down, and took the steepest part of the road in strides. She didn't even both to look up at the window. Once around the dark corner of the house, she began to climb the ladder.

Dear Catriona [Anne wrote]
I hope you are not reading this next month. My dad is just a chancer. Don't worry about him. I expect you are all right, but I think you are probably braver than I am. I fancy myself a bit but I would never do things that had no chance of getting through, just for the hell of it (pardon my French).

I hope I see you tomorrow.
Love always,

Anne

P.S. I don't know if I want to be called The Keeper of Crystalcant. I think I would rather be called something like Black Lightning.

P.P.S. You are the only friend I've ever had.

As you read

A reading log

Keep a log which records your impressions of each story in
A Girl's Best Friend as you read. View your reading log as a
kind of diary, where you can note down feelings and
thoughts as they occur to you. It should provide plenty of
ideas for coursework assignments later on.

In your reading log, aim to:

Record key events, perhaps critical moments in each story
which make an impression on you.

Ask questions about aspects of plot, character, setting,
themes and the style of writing which you find puzzling,
or intriguing.

Reminisce about experiences and memories of your own,
sparked off by your reading.

Compare each story with another in the anthology or with
one you have read elsewhere.

Predict what is going to happen at key moments in each
story and say why you think this.

Reflect upon some of the ideas, themes, thoughts and
feelings expressed and give your reactions to them.

Comment on any aspects of a story's style – that is, the
variety of ways in which language is used to tell each
story.

Assess how much you are enjoying each story, how
interesting you find it, and whether or not you would
recommend it to other readers, giving your reasons.

If you intend to study the stories individually, the assignments from p. 150 onwards in this section will help you to
do so. If you intend to read and study the anthology as a
whole, turn to the assignments in **After reading**
on pp. 164–167. Whatever your approach, you may wish to
keep a reading log recording your impressions of *A Girl's
Best Friend*.

Funny How Time Flies

Role-playing

How is Kim affected by the news of her parents' impending divorce? Reread the story up to the point where Kim pays her visit to Bess, and note down all the signs you can find that she is upset. Share your findings in groups.

Now imagine the scene *before* the story begins, when Kim and her brother, Duane, are given the news of their parents' divorce. Taking the roles of Kim, Duane, mother and father, act out this scene showing how the parents announce the news, and how their son and daughter react to it.

Story extension

Imagine that Kim invites Bess to her house for tea. Bess and her mother meet for the first time. Write an extension to the story as if you are Kim, narrating how the two women exchange views on the subject of marriage and divorce. Suppose that Bess has intended to say little, but finds this quite impossible . . .

In the original story, Kim narrates with a dry, ironic wit. Aim to use a similar approach to bring out the comic possibilities of the encounter between the two women.

Personal writing

Do you ever find your mind so full of thoughts that you are unable to fall asleep? Drawing on your own experiences or on imaginary ones, write about your thoughts as you lie awake. Show how each thought appears, then disappears, how new thoughts take over, and how niggling worries prevent you from relaxing into sleep.

Reread pp. 3–4, and use a similar style to the one here. For example, describe what you are thinking in the present tense using short sentences, abrupt subject changes, and snatches of remembered conversation.

Always Remembered

Studying style

The story is narrated in three ways. There is the third-person narrative; there are the diary letters to the imaginary friend, Teresa; and there are extracts of poetry.

In pairs, discuss why you think the story is told in three different ways. How does each way of narrating influence your view of Sam's death?

Personal writing

Recall a time in your past which remains vividly in your memory. Perhaps look at a photo album to remind you of this time in your life. Then take any of the following suggestions, or an idea of your own, and write your own story using at least two different styles – in the same way as *Always Remembered*:

- an accident in which you were involved
- the loss of someone you cared for
- moving house/leaving your country
- getting a pet, and losing it
- an ill-fated holiday

Newspaper report

Draft and write a report on the death of Dee's father as it might appear in the local newspaper. Consider how outsiders might view Dee's father and the causes of his death.

Try to give this story an eye-catching headline, and a particular 'angle'. Your report might include eye-witness accounts by people who saw him lying on the pavement, as well as interviews with the people who knew him: Dee, Dee's mother, Anastasia, Mr Rose.

Lily

Talking in pairs

In pairs, describe what it is like to meet someone you have not seen for a very long time. It might be an old friend from your days at primary school; a relative or friend of your parents; perhaps a teacher. Discuss whether people match your expectations when you see them again and whether they change.

Is there anybody from the past whom you would be curious to see again?

Role-playing

In groups, imagine you are guests at the Waites' New Year's Eve Party. Choose one person in the group to be Lily. Start by making party conversation, then ask 'Lily' to make an entrance. As the story describes, go silent, then resume your conversation again. Before you start the role-play, ask yourselves:

- What might the party guests be saying about Lily?
- How much do they really know about her?

Aim to make your party conversation as gossipy as possible, mixing details given in the story with your own ideas.

Lily's point of view

Retell the story as if you are Lily, starting with the meeting in the hairdresser's salon. How quickly do you realise that Jill is Ralph Waite's daughter? Did you really have an affair with him? If so, what became of this relationship?

In your version, clarify the mystery of Lily's relationship with Jill's father, revealing how innocent or scheming you really are. Describe your impressions of the New Year's Eve Party and of meeting Jill there.

Sunni

Interviewing eye-witnesses

In groups, set up a series of interviews between the reporter of a national newspaper and certain people involved in the Southall riots. If you choose the role of reporter, your main aim is to hear different points of view of the incident. If you choose to be interviewed, aim to give an eye-witness account of what you saw, as well as a clear opinion of how the trouble started and who is to blame.

You might choose to be: Sunni, Firoz, Kriji, Briji, a police officer, a local shop keeper, a National Front member, a doctor on the scene, or an old person passing by.

Reread the description of the riots. If possible, tape record and then play back the interviews to your class.

Writing a newspaper report

Write a newspaper report for a chosen national newspaper. Decide how you intend to present your report:

- as a balanced account which represents the viewpoints of both police and demonstrators?
- as a biased account in favour of *one* viewpoint?

The terms you use will show the 'angle' of your report. For example, demonstrators can be seen either as 'victims of police brutality' or as 'rioters' who 'threaten law and order'.

Filming a short story

If this was a film, she'd be crying . . .   p. 42

Life was lived through films for Sunni and her friends before the Southall riots. Work out how you might make the story itself into a film. To help you:

1 Make a record of the main dates and events which occur in the story, spanning three years from 1976 to 1979.
2 Decide on the emphasis of the film. For example, do you wish to focus on Sunni's relationship with Firoz? or the political events leading up to the Southall riots?
3 Note down how the story might be divided into a series of scenes. Then produce a film script for a single scene which you consider to be central to the film. (Follow the directions given on p. 167.)

First Foot

Discussing the title

How much do you know about the Scottish tradition of 'first footing'? Find out as much as you can both about what it signifies and what it involves.

What is the significance of the title to the story?

Role-playing

Tensions can occur between brothers and sisters for various reasons. In *First Foot* the narrator feels that her sister, Irene, has turned their mother against her. In groups, work out a role-play based on one of these sources of tension:

- a parent takes the side of your brother/sister and against you
- a parent buys your brother/sister something, but not you
- your brother/sister 'tells tales' about you
- your brother/sister refuses to share something with you

Try acting out the scene in two different ways. Make the first version aggressive and confrontational, and make the second reasonable and conciliatory. Does either approach help to resolve the problem?

An alternative ending

Imagine that this story does not end in the desperate way that it does, with Janice gathering her things together to leave home. Take up the story at the point when Mammy says on p. 59:

'Where the hell have you been?'

Perhaps drawing on your work for 'Role-playing' above, think of ways in which Janice might have defused the tension in the house and managed to talk reasonably with her mother and sister.

Irene's point of view

Retell this story as if you are the narrator's sister, Irene. Use all the details in the story to help you build up a picture of her. In your version, show the life Irene leads, how she views her mother and sister, and why she behaves as she does.

Once Upon A Time

Talking in pairs

'You're always dreaming, that's your trouble . . .'   p. 64

Make a note of all the things Elizabeth dreams of in the story. Then, in pairs, discuss how you might complete the wording of these two sentences:

- It *is* healthy for Elizabeth to dream in her life because . . .
- It is *un*healthy for Elizabeth to dream in her life because . . .

Which statement do you feel more inclined to support, and why?

Personal writing

Using the same approach as *Once Upon A Time*, write a story about your own life, in which you describe a fantasy and compare it with a typical experience in your own life. You might draw on one of the following situations:

- having an accident
- shopping for clothes
- entering a competition
- meeting someone at the beach/swimming pool/shopping centre
- getting into a fight.

If you wish to write in a similar style to the original, aim to make the humour dry, low-key and ironic. Also try to avoid an obvious ending. For example, think of alternatives to the 'happily ever after' ending.

Adapting a fairy tale

Choose a folk or fairy tale which is familiar to you and write a modern version of that tale, either drawing on your own experiences or taking a current 'story' from the news. Use the same approach as 'Once Upon A Time', interweaving your telling of the original tale with the modern version.

Dreaming

Group discussion

In groups, discuss whether or not you agree with the following statements about dreams, giving your reasons:

1 Everybody dreams.
2 Dreams are just meaningless, random images.
3 Dreams are in black and white, not colour.
4 Dreams can be prophetic: they can foretell the future.
5 Most people have recurring dreams.
6 Dreams can tell us about people's true feelings.

Understanding

How good are you at interpreting dreams? In pairs, look again at the first few pages of *Dreaming*, where Donna's dream is described in some detail. Using your reading of the whole story to help you, discuss the significance of:

- the 'vaguely familiar' room
- the yellow lamp bathing the room in light
- the strong impression of colour, light, smells and sound outside the room
- the room filled with shadowy figures
- calling out and not being heard
- seeing the figure of herself in the room
- her desperation to return to the room and failure to do so.

What indications are there in the story that Donna's journey 'Back Home' may be more than just a dream?

Keeping a dream diary

Consider keeping a diary of the dreams you have during one week. The best approach is to write down everything you can remember about a dream the minute you wake up – not an easy thing to do! Don't worry if your notes are haphazard and confused – dreams are like this too. Our memory of dreams often fades in the very act of making sense of them.

Gentle Persuasion

Pair work

In the story, Rachel uses a variety of 'gentle' methods to persuade her sister to lend her a dress. In pairs, note down each method of persuasion Rachel uses in the course of the conversation, and find a phrase to describe this method. For example:

Arousing curiosity: e.g. 'I'm going to a party tonight.'

Role-playing

In pairs, with a third person observing you, take turns to role-play any of the situations below. Ask the observer to note down which methods are being used by the person in the persuading role. Try to persuade:

- a friend to accompany you on a blind date
- a friend to lend you a record/some money
- a parent to let you stay out late on Saturday night
- a teacher to let you have an extension on a coursework assignment
- a brother/sister to run an errand for you
- a parent to let you go on a school skiing trip/camping holiday with some friends.

When you have finished the role-plays, discuss which methods of persuasion seemed to be most effective, and which least, in achieving what you wanted.

An alternative version

Write an alternative version of this story, in which you imagine that Judy has no intention of lending her sister the dress. Develop the dialogue into an angry confrontation between the two. Decide how the matter might resolve itself – with one or the other backing down? in a stalemate? with both sisters realising that they have to be more reasonable and reach a compromise?

Changes

Pair work

In *Changes*, Marcia and Danny are expected to behave in rather different ways by their parents.

- In pairs, list any instances in your own experience of how parents expect their sons and daughters to behave differently.
- Find all the instances in *Changes* of how Marcia is expected to behave differently from her brother, and is therefore treated differently.

Discuss whether you feel that there are occasions when parents are justified in treating sons and daughters differently.

Role-playing

At the end of the story, Marcia has resolved to move out of her parents' home and find a job.

In groups, discuss what might happen when Marcia decides to tell her parents of her decision to leave home. Work out two possible scenes. For example, in the first, imagine that Marcia is able to persuade her parents that leaving home is a good thing, but in the second . . .

Now allocate the parts of Marcia, her parents, and possibly Danny or Steve. Act out the two versions of the scene to other members of your class, and ask them to judge which is the more convincing.

Letter to a problem page

'You have parents who love you . . . you have no problems.'
p. 96

Despite Sandra's comment, Marcia is discontented with her life at home. Imagine that she decides to write to the problem page of a teenage magazine for advice. As Marcia, write a letter describing your problems at a particular moment in the story, and explaining why you feel unable to resolve them.

Then, taking the role of the magazine's 'agony aunt', either write a reply to your own letter, or, better still, swap your letter with a partner's and write a reply to it.

Day Out

A taped reading

In groups, work out a reading of the scene in which Val and Lisa meet Vic and Gazzer. First, decide at which points in the story your scene should open and close, then decide who will read the narrative and who will read the speeches of each character.

Try to convey the exuberance and wicked sense of humour of the two girls on a day out, as well as the awkwardness of the two boys who are overwhelmed by the girls' teasing.

When you have practised a reading of the scene, make a tape-recording of it and play it back to other members of your class.

An alternative version

In groups, work out an alternative version to the scene in which Val and Lisa meet Vic and Gazzer. In your own version, show how the two boys stand up to the taunts of the two girls. Decide how the boys succeed in making fools of the girls: by bullying them? by making jokes at their expense? by charming them?

Develop your scene into either a role-play, or a radio script which you tape record.

The opening of a television play

Imagine that you are to advise an independent television director who wishes to rewrite *Day Out* as a television play for a young adult audience. Your particular task is to suggest how the play should begin. The director has asked you to emphasise three themes: the jealousy Val feels towards her friend; the forlorn setting of a run-down holiday town at low-season; and the comic possibilities of a girls' day out.

Work out how you envisage the television play will open, drawing closely on the beginning of 'Day Out'. Then follow the directions given on p. 167, to write your television script.

Seeing For Herself

Group discussion

Discuss in groups whether you would agree or disagree with these statements about the short story:

- Rukmini is far too sentimental about the poverty she sees in India.
- Aunt Pushpa's view is right: 'Everyone works hard in their own way. Everyone has their own trials and tribulations.'
- India is shown to have one rule for the rich and another for the poor.
- Rukmini's inheritance money would have been wasted on Acchaamma.
- While her parents are with her, Rukmini is unable 'to see for herself'.

Writing a poem

What disturbs you about the world we live in? Think of the issues you have strong feelings about and why this is. Try to express these thoughts by writing a poem or speech which includes some of these opening lines:

I live in a world I do not
  always like . . .
I am saddened by . . .
I feel angered by . . .
I am frightened by . . .

But if I must live here . . .
I will protest about . . .
I will fight for . . .
I will support people who . . .

Acchaamma's point of view

Tell the story of Rukmini's visit to India as if you are Acchaamma. Write this as a monologue – as if you are speaking to a friend. In your story, indicate what you think and feel about:

- your role as family bread-winner
- the friendliness of Rukmini towards you
- the conversation with Rukmini's mother about 'plans' for the future
- the gift of food – and later, money – from the family.

In your account, show whether Acchaamma is a downtrodden woman without plans for the future, or whether she is timid for other reasons.

Aran Sweater

Group discussion

Have you ever had to stay in hospital? In groups, describe any experiences you may have had, then give your impressions of hospital life. You might comment on:

- the daily timetable of events
- the medical attention
- the other patients
- the friends and acquaintances you made
- the visiting times

How well did you adapt to hospital life? How ready were you to leave? Discuss whether the impressions of hospitals you receive from television serials are true to life.

Role-playing

What must it be like for people like Flo and Mrs Rice, the two old women in the story, who spend a long time in hospital? Consider how they might begin to lose contact with the world outside, as they adjust to the routines of hospital life.

In pairs, improvise a conversation between the two ladies *after* Jen has left hospital. In your conversation refer to Jen's visit and her Aran sweater. What significance might this sweater have for Flo and Mrs Rice?

Writing a diary entry

Imagine you are a person who spends some time in a hospital. For example, you might be:

- one of the characters in the story
- somebody you know well who is a nurse, porter, doctor, cook
- yourself, remembering a past experience as a patient.

In your diary, record a typical day or night in hospital, showing how life is dominated by set routines which may be upset or highlighted by emergencies.

Well, Well, Well

Role-playing

In pairs, improvise one or two scenes where the roles between parent and child are reversed, as they are in the story. Choose from this list, or use an idea of your own. For example, imagine that either your father or mother has:

- taken up a danger sport
- had an irresponsible spending spree
- gone out for the night and returned late
- bought clothes for a wedding which are unsuitable
- is mixing with friends you do not approve of.

Consider how to give small clues to the parent's identity *before* the final punchline – for example, the parent may have a more adult style of speech. Either tape record your role-play, or perform it before members of your class.

Writing a dialogue

Think of any pair of roles where there is a strong convention for one person to be in authority, and the other to be subordinate or dependent. For example:

- teacher/pupil
- sergeant major/private soldier
- doctor/patient
- older/younger brother, and/or sister
- Samaritan/person in need of help.

Write a humorous dialogue between this pair where the roles are unexpectedly reversed and the ending is a surprise. Use the same style and approach as *Well, Well, Well*.

The Night Run

Story telling

There are many kinds of science fiction story and the Crosstan story is of a certain type. In pairs, note down some of the features of this type of science fiction from your reading of *The Night Run* and perhaps from your own reading. For example, one feature might be people taking the disguise of wild animals.

Using the features you have noted, make up another story of the Crosstan type. Tell your story to another pair, making it as dramatic as possible.

Diagram of the double plot

The Night Run has a double plot. Working in pairs, find all the links between the Crosstan story and the 'real-life' story of Catriona's friendship with Anne. For example, 'the night run' has a significance in *both* stories. Using a chart like the one below, note each link in the order in which it happens:

CROSSTAN	'REAL LIFE'
1. Sorceress taunts Cathoren	Two boys bully Catriona

Now design a large diagram which shows the main episodes in the two stories, and indicates the links between these episodes. Make a wall display of the diagrams so that you can compare your version with other people's.

Writing a 'double plot' story

Imagine you have a nightmare about some danger which may threaten one of your friends. The dream suggests that only *you* can save your friend from danger. Describe the nightmare, using the language and imagery of a Crosstan story. Show how the message of your dream applies to 'real life' by telling the story of what you do when you wake up.

You can either tell the two stories in sequence – first the nightmare, then the 'real-life' story, or (like *The Night Run*) you can interweave the two stories.

After reading

The coursework assignments here are based on your reading of the whole anthology. They offer suggestions for extended study, project work and comparative essays. Please read Christina Dunhill's introduction again before starting an assignment – it may provide some useful resource material.

1 Write a book review of *A Girl's Best Friend* for readers of your own age. The aim of your review is to give your impressions of this anthology of short stories, and to explain whether you would recommend it or not. In your review, consider:

- the main themes covered by the stories – e.g. friendship between girls
- the way girls and women are presented – e.g. positively, as strong, independent people making choices?
- stories you particularly enjoyed, with your reasons
- stories you did not enjoy and why this was
- the writing style: how varied, accessible, original, entertaining?
- which age/type of reader the stories would appeal to

2 Imagine that a television director is hoping to select *six* of the stories from *A Girl's Best Friend* for a series of short plays for teenage viewers. The title of the series is to be *A Girl's Choice*. The director has written to your school to ask for advice on which stories from the anthology young people would recommend.

Choose the six stories from the anthology which you feel could be best adapted to television and would fit the series title. Make notes on why you have chosen each of the six stories, and say how you envisage each story might be adapted for television.

3 Friendship between two girls, or between girls and women, is portrayed as a source of both support and conflict in the anthology. In *Funny How Time Flies* and *Aran Sweater*, an old lady is able to help a young girl overcome problems in her life. In *Day Out*, a girl is jealous of her best friend's holiday romance, but is relieved to find that it has not affected their friendship.

Choose several stories from the anthology and compare the various types of friendship between girls and women. Drawing on your own experience, say how important you think such friendships are.

4 The relationship between young people and their parents can often be difficult and unpredictable. When friction occurs, it is not always obvious who is to blame. For example, in *Changes*, Marcia feels stifled by her parents' overprotective love; in *First Foot*, Janice no longer feels welcome at home.

Choose any *three* of the stories you have read in this anthology, and contrast the relationships between parents and their daughters.

5 Growing up can often be a harsh and unsettling time. Sunni recalls how the films she saw were more real to her than life itself, *until* she experienced racial violence. In *Seeing For Herself*, Rukmini is shocked to discover people's indifference to poverty and inequality in India.

Choose any *three* stories in the anthology where the main character experiences events which force her to view life differently. Compare the ways in which each story shows the difficulties of growing up.

6 Several stories in the anthology show how teenage girls become suffocated by the tedium of everyday life and long for some kind of escape. In *Once Upon A Time*, Elizabeth daydreams that she is a wealthy, successful and a beautiful woman. In *The Night Run* Catriona turns to the fantasy of science fiction stories to make life more exciting.

Choose *three* or more of the stories from the anthology, and compare the fantasy lives of each character. Do you believe that fantasy is a harmless escape route from the pressures of everyday life?

7 *The funny stories are . . . serious. The serious stories have their comic moments.*
Do you believe that you can write about serious matters in a humorous way? Choose any *three* stories from the anthology where there is a blend of humour and a serious theme. By close reference, discuss whether the use of humour helps the reader to appreciate, or dismiss the serious messages in each story.

8 What do you think are the qualities which make a good short story? A surprising or thought-provoking ending? A character with whom you can identify?

Make a list of all the features you think are important. Then write an appraisal of *A Girl's Best Friend* in which you judge which stories are successful by your criteria and which are not.

Appendix

Writing a film or television script

Here are some working guidelines for producing a script for sound and camera:

1 Use a larger version of the form below to give directions for camera shots, and a description of what is on the sound track at any given time.

2 The sound track is likely to be mainly dialogue with some music and sound effects. Consider whether or not you will use a narrator as a 'voice over', who explains the links between scenes.

3 Use sketches (line drawings or stick people will do) to show the subject of each visual frame. Number each frame in sequence.

4 To show the camera movements between each visual frame, use the standard coding:

CU	Close-up (face or detail)
FI	Fade-in
FO	Fade-out
LS	Long-shot (group or scene in total)
MCU	Medium close-up (face and half body)
PAN	Pan (swing camera around a scene)
ZI/ZO	Zoom in/Zoom out

No.	Visual	Camera Shot	Sound
1			
2			